OUTDOOR SCULPTURE
in Grand Rapids

FAY L. HENDRY

photography by Balthazar Korab

ιota press
Okemos, Michigan

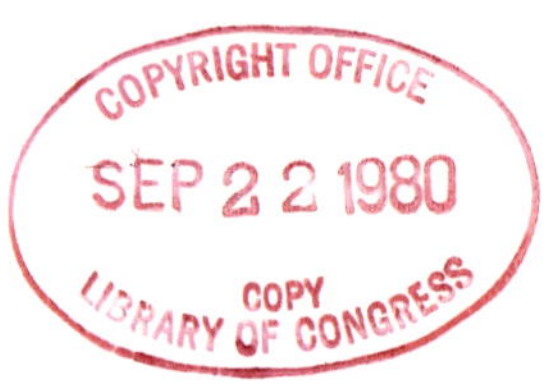

Designed by Dorris E. Birchfield, Michigan State University

Typesetting by Superior Graphics, Lansing, Michigan

Printed by Thomson-Shore, Inc., Dexter, Michigan

Library of Congress Cataloging in Publication Data

Hendry, Fay L. 1937-
Outdoor sculpture in Grand Rapids.
Bibliography: p.
Includes index.
1. Sculpture—Michigan—Grand Rapids—Guide-books.
2. Grand Rapids—Monuments—Guide-books. 3. Grand Rapids—Statues—Guide-books. I. Korab, Balthazar. II. Title.
NB235.G7H46 917.74′560443 80-7500
ISBN 0-936412-00-3

FRONT COVER: Alexander Calder, *La Grande Vitesse*

BACK COVER: Detail, Metz Building Reliefs

CONTENTS

PREFACE

My interest in Michigan sculpture began in 1976 when I was hired by the Michigan History Division, Department of State, to prepare a report on cultural properties for the Coastal Zone Management Program. I intended to include information on sculpture, but when I checked possible sources, I found that practically no information was available. I was told that this wasn't New York or Washington and that there was no information because there was no sculpture.

I wondered if there were sculpture but no information, and began a study of outdoor sculpture in Lansing. Much to my surprise, there was more in the city than I or anyone else had been aware of. While much of what I recorded was not of high aesthetic merit, the sculpture yielded interesting information about the social and cultural history of Lansing. It revealed a city which neither had developed a strong sense of community identity nor had maximized its cultural potential.

The study also revealed the need to create an awareness of and appreciation for sculpture. With awareness and appreciation, there is the potential to enrich our social and cultural heritage and to influence the heritage of future generations. For sculpture not only reflects a community but contributes to it as well. It provokes sensual and intellectual responses, and it records and celebrates the human presence. It is a thread that stitches together the fabric of the past, the present, and the future.

The Lansing study led to slide presentations, tours, a television program, and a photographic exhibition, *Outdoor Sculpture in Greater Lansing: From Tombstones to Titus the Tinner,* which was held at the Michigan Historical Museum from June through December of 1977, the Society for the Study of Midwestern Literature in 1978, and the Honors College at Michigan State University in 1979. The Lansing study also led to the present expanded project, *Outdoor Sculpture in Grand Rapids, Kalamazoo, and Lansing, Michigan,* which began in 1978. Sculpture located and documented in all three cities served as the basis for the preparation of three separate guidebooks and a photographic exhibition. A public forum on outdoor sculpture will be coordinated with the exhibition which will travel to each city during 1980.

A field inventory was completed for each city of all the sculptural expressions. Free-standing, cemetery, and architectural sculpture was included regardless of aesthetic merit. A cross section of sculpture has been selected from the inventory for the guidebook with an orientation toward social and cultural history rather than aesthetic merit. Both the work of artisan and artist has been included with no intent to obscure the distinction, to disservice art, or to discourage a critical evaluation of the works.

The purpose of the guidebook is to create an awareness of outdoor sculpture in Grand Rapids and to serve as guide and an enticement to actually experience these works. For sculpture is best understood and evaluated when experienced. Entries are brief for this reason.

Entries were also limited in some cases by the constraints of time, money, and accessibility of materials. The research data which have been generated by this project will be housed in the Michigan State University Archives and Historical Collections. It is hoped that this publication will elicit further information about these works and artists. Additional information and corrections are welcomed by the author and may be sent to ιota press, 2749 E. Mt. Hope Road, Okemos, Michigan 48864.

Please note that the date for each sculpture entry refers to the time the work was created and may not necessarily refer to the date commissioned or dedicated. Dimensions refer to height and bracketed information refers to inscriptions. The biographical information for each artist, which includes additional works and their dates when available, has been accepted as given. Sculpture that is mentioned but not illustrated is indicated by a °.

Fay L. Hendry
October 18, 1979

ACKNOWLEDGMENTS

Outdoor Sculpture in Grand Rapids, Kalamazoo, and Lansing, Michigan, could not have been carried out without the help of Professor Eldon N. Van Liere, Michigan State University, and Professor Ronald Watson, Director of the Urban Institute for Contemporary Art and Chairperson of the Art Department, Aquinas College. Cooperation was also given by Fred A. Myers, former Director of the Grand Rapids Art Museum; Harry Greaver, former Director, and Thomas A. Kayser, current Director, Kalamazoo Institute of Arts; and Michael J. Smith, Chief, Michigan Historical Museum (State Museum), Lansing.

Funds for the project were provided by the Michigan State University Development Fund, the Michigan Council for the Arts, the Grand Rapids Foundation, the Kalamazoo Foundation, an anonymous Lansing donor, the Michigan Foundation for the Arts, and the Michigan Council for the Humanities.

Help has also been provided by many individuals and I apologize to anyone whose name has been omitted from the following list: Jack Abbring, John Alford, Earl Van Alsburg, William Battjes, Gerald A. Bax, William Boorstein, Diane Boozer, Leslie Bradshaw, Erling B. Brauner, Nancy J. Brown, Mrs. Harry Colton, Mrs. Ralph W. Demmon, Doris Doherty, Joyce Dwyer, Roger Funk, Weldon Frankforter, Williard Dean Goodlin, the staff of the Grand Rapids Art Museum, Leon C. Gray, Gloria Gregory, Linda Halsey, Richard Hathaway, Jerry Hazzard, Herbert E. Hendry, Sister Marie Heyda, Thomas Heywood, Robert E. Hicks, Allan Hollingsworth, Fred Honhart, Ruth Hornbach, June Horowitz, Gerrit Huitsing, Robert Julien, Lee M. Hutchins, Dave Jensen, Luise Johnson, Dorothy Judd, Mary Ann Keeler, Mike Keeler, Luci King, Ellen Kinnebrew, Elizabeth Knapp, Charles Killgoar, F. W. Knecht, George Kooistra, Mrs. George Kranenberg, Henry Lathrop, John Luyendyk, Rupert McGinn, Catherine Madsen, Susan Marshall, Susan Quaintance Mason, Sister John Marie, Cindy Marsh, Mrs. Hugh J. Meeter, the staff of the Michigan Room, Grand Rapids Public Library,

Gale Most, Nancy Mulnix, Robert Murdock, Dennis Nawrocki, Cindy Newman, Richard Oele, Gordon Olson, Connie Oosting, James Oosting, Gary Post, William Pries, Barbara Roelofs, Ilene Schechter, James Sharp, Edward A. Skendzel, Lucija Skuja, Scott S. Smith, Craig Staudenbaur, Marjorie Staudenbaur, Shirlee Studt, Richard E. Sullivan, William Thrall, Chester Trout, Laurie Vander Stoep, Douglas Vander Wall, John Van Haver, James Vermeulen, Linda Wagner, Karen Watson, Mrs. George Whinery, Calvin Wieringa, and Evelyn Wisner. I am, of course, indebted to all the artists both living and dead who are the substance of this project.

FOREWORD

The public sculpture, researched and catalogued almost single-handedly by Fay Hendry and masterfully photographed by Balthazar Korab, presented in this guide documents the works in this community which have survived from the past and those which are being created today. The old sculptures are familiar for they have been around a long time, but they have become remote in meaning, and much of the most modern of sculpture seems remote by design. Public sculpture has never had an easy time of it, for it is asked to do the impossible—to please a wide diversity of tastes and interests. The very fact that it is public and thereby unavoidable tends to make it controversial.

In the past public sculpture, whether it served to decorate a building or was a freestanding work, served very clear humanizing purposes. More often than not the intent was didactic, and when it was not, as in the case of an ornamental carving, its purpose was to give the eye a moment of delight. Modern taste has done much to obscure these monuments from the past with the exception of those sacred precincts where we have buried the past and collected monuments to the dead. Beyond these hallowed grounds the market place takes over, and the monuments that dominate are huge impersonal buildings of a democratic sameness lacking, or nearly so, that humanizing touch of decorative sculpture. The older buildings which survive and do have some sculpture adorning them seem either quaint or too unique to exist comfortably with the shivering towers of steel and glass that surround them. It is as if these reminders of past individualism are threats to a predominant concept of equality and sameness.

If modern architecture has left little room for the decorative or allegorical relief on its surfaces, it has completely dwarfed the freestanding sculpture both old and new. To be sure, man has been made puny by much of modern architecture, but we for the most part accommodate ourselves to it; however, should that urban pedestrian look up and take note of some sculpture dwarfed by monuments to commerce and politics, he or she might be struck by how scale and space have changed in the twentieth century. The old sculpture may have been preserved, but very often its setting has not, and the sculpture comes out the loser. Much of modern sculpture has adopted an industrial tone with its use of polished chrome-like surfaces or sheet steel, rusted or painted, welded or bolted together allowing for a scale that can attempt to compete with huge buildings in a vernacular common with them and be eye-catching in the midst of an urban bustle.

Modern sculpture with its concerns for pure form has the potential of universality. Pure form can be understood by all and/or be moving to all; but, despite this potential, it is, nevertheless, found incomprehensible by many. Pure form does not read like a bronze figure of a dancing young woman draped in garlands of flowers representing Spring. To the viewer with an eye for pure form the very pose of such a figure with its tensions and balances may be most satisfying, but the allegorical aspect is a distraction. On the other hand, the message of Spring's celebration of a liberation from winter and the hope for the fertile months ahead as well as a comprehensible technical skill at rendering a likeness are understandable to all. Thus, there is in the dancing maiden a community comprehension on a multitude of levels denied by many modern works despite their "universality." Sculpture free of representation and allegory in search of purity can be and has come to be appreciated or accepted by many, but it does not serve to reinforce any vision of public values other than the belief that art has a place in public life and in some general way is uplifting and enriching.

This guidebook is an attempt to help us all pause as we hurry by and take note of how one generation sought to speak to another without asking us to go into a museum or pore over a book. The illustrations herein isolate the sculpture as much as possible from the competing and often overwhelming surrounding distractions to help direct our eyes to what we have here and perhaps inspire us to make public sculpture a meaningful expression of our own time.

Eldon N. Van Liere

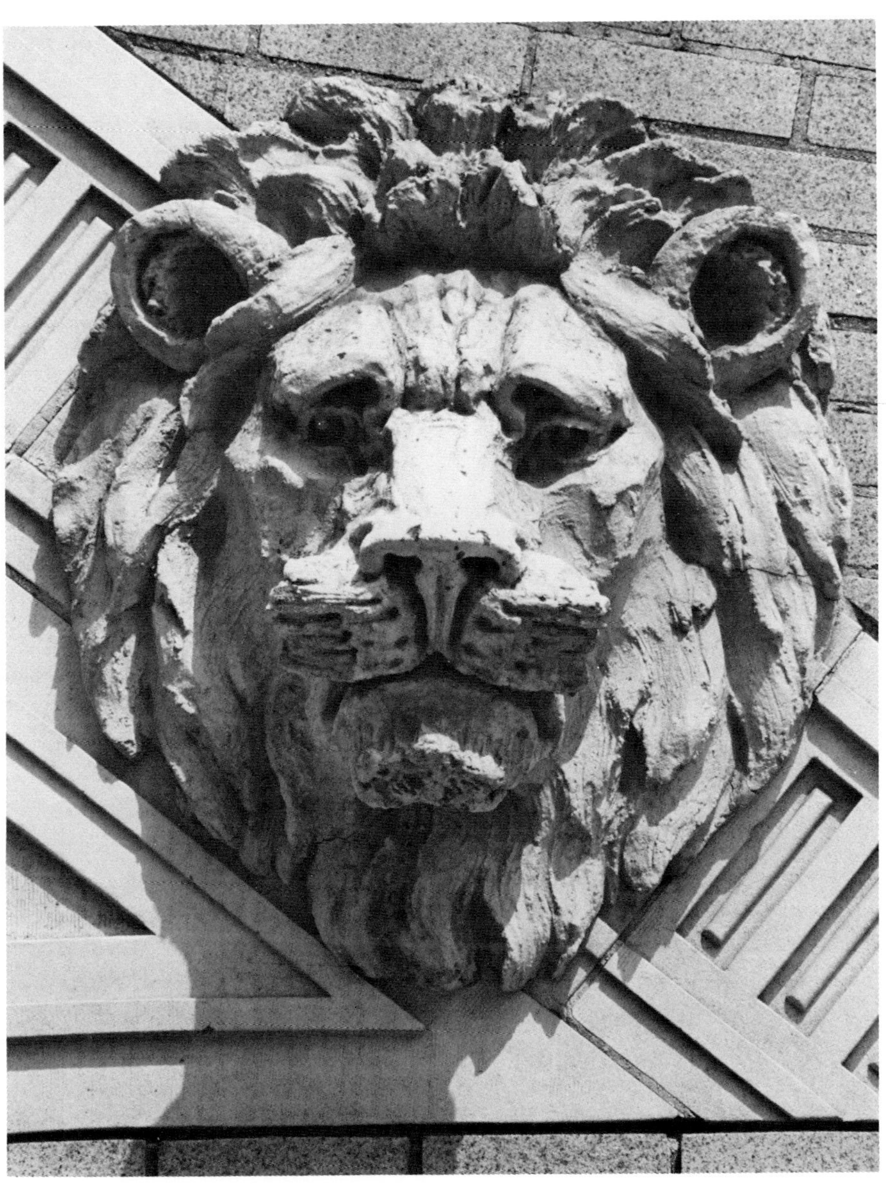

Detail, Heystek Building (A-10, p. 37).

OUTDOOR SCULPTURE IN GRAND RAPIDS

By the 1830s Michigan was ripe for statehood. The fur trade was peaking, the Indians had ceded most of their lands, and transporation was greatly facilitated by the construction of arteries like the Erie Canal and the Old Sauk Trail (U.S. 12). Land speculators and settlers, primarily from New England and New York, began streaming into the territory.

By the time Michigan achieved statehood in 1837, there were already a considerable number of settlers living at the site of Grand Rapids in an otherwise sparsely populated part of the state. Two of the earliest settlers were Reverend Issac McCoy and Louis Campau. McCoy, who established the Baptist Thomas Mission on the west side of the Grand River in 1825, first came to the area in 1823 to establish contact with the Indians who lived along the Grand River. Campau, a fur trader, set up his trading post in 1826 on the opposite side of the river near the present day location of Campau Square. Campau platted the Village of Grand Rapids in 1831, taking the name from the nearby rapids.

A portion of this land was sold to Lucius Lyon, a surveyor, who proceeded to plat the Village of Kent in 1832. Lyon named his plat the Village of Kent after Kent County. Established in 1831, the county was named after Chancellor James Kent of New York State. Lyon, whose name can still be found on one of the village streets, was born in Shelburne, Vermont. After serving as one of the first congressional senators from Michigan, Lyon established a home in Grand Rapids in 1839, one year after the settlement officially became a village. It is to these two men, and in particular to the stubborn Campau, that the city owes its angled downtown streets. The early settlers also changed the face of the area, which came to be known as "Grab Corners" after the Civil War, by cutting away Prospect Hill to use as fill around the islands in the Grand River.

It is not known for certain when the first sculptor or stone carver came to Grand Rapids, though a stone carver likely followed the settlers to carve the inevitable grave marker. Albert Baxter, author of the *History of the City of Grand Rapids, Michigan,* (1891), states that

> Daniel S. T. Weller in 1848 brought into the village a small stock of Vermont marble, and opened a shop near the foot of Monroe street, for the manufacture of grave stones, monuments, table tops, mantels, and other similar work pertaining to the marble cutter's trade. The demand at that time was small, and only for the plainest and simplest of work, orders for elaborate carving being very rare; but, being the first, and the only one of its kind then in the place, this shop furnished fairly remunerative employment for two or three workmen (pp. 489-490).

The early marble slabs repeat many of the motifs which were used in the East. Winged angels, roses, weeping willows, all commenting on the life and death cycle, offered solace to those who mourned and new life in heaven for those who had died. Besides grave markers, stone carvers sometimes carved civic monuments in direct competition with sculptors. They sometimes also collaborated with a sculptor by carving the pedestal for a work or by translating the sculptor's model into stone. This was the case with Grand Rapids monument maker Frank D. Black who collaborated with Pompeo Coppini on several commissions, including the *John Ball Memorial* (1925) [p. 96] located in the park which bears Ball's name.

Ball, another of Grand Rapids' early settlers plays a leading role in Lumen Winter's relief the *Legend of Grand Rapids* (1976) [p. 55]. Winter's frieze chronicles the history of Grand Rapids from its earliest beginnings to the present. Corrado Joseph Parducci's Indian and other reliefs (1926) [p. 35] on the Michigan National Bank also portray the early history of Grand Rapids.

The lively beginnings of Grand Rapids are characterized by the city motto, *Motu Viget,* which was adopted by the city fathers along with the city seal when Grand Rapids passed from a village to a city in 1850. Freely translated, the motto means "strength through activity." It was the city motto that inspired the title for Mark di Suvero's recent *Motu* (1977) [p. 21]. Reliefs of the city seal can be found on the Filter Plant

(c. 1912) [p. 83]; in an elegant cartouche above the original doorway of the Grand Rapids Public Library (1902-1904)°; and over the doorway of the Grand Rapids Public Museum (c. 1939)°.

By the end of the Civil War, communities in the Midwest had begun to improve and beautify their cities. Substantial and elegant buildings sprang up alongside or replaced earlier modest ones. Among such buildings is Saint James Church, whose facade carries heads that were quite likely carved by a local stone carver from local sandstone (c. 1872) [p. 93]. The heads, possibly of Saint James the Greater, appear to be the earliest extant sculptural works in Grand Rapids other than grave markers. This church was originally constructed for a predominately Irish Catholic parish, but other nationalities were also adding flavor to the city including the Dutch, Germans, Poles, and Lithuanians.

Many of the later churches, which serve as focal points for the various religious groups, are articulated with sculpture. Examples of sculpture on two of the Polish Catholic churches are the Gandola Brothers' Angels with Golden Trumpets, Saint Adalbert (c. 1910) [p. 90] and the tympanum reliefs of the *Nativity, Crucifixion,* and *Ascension* over the doorways to Sacred Heart Church (c. 1922) [p. 95]. The tradition of the Dutch Reformed Church of placing a rooster on top of their buildings has been kept alive with B. Wathof and Sons' Rooster Weathervane, Central Reformed Church (1957) [p. 71]. One of Grand Rapids' earliest religious establishments was the above-mentioned Baptist Thomas Mission, predecessor to Fountain Street Church. Now interdenominational, the present building is covered with an extensive sculptural program (c. 1922) [p. 49].

In addition to Saint James Church, many other substantial buildings with sculptural decoration were erected after the Civil War. Surprisingly, the first City Hall was not constructed until 1885. When Elijah E. Myers' design was completed in 1888, two bronze maidens flanked the Lyon Street entrance°. In 1969, the building was razed to make way for Vandenburg Center, an urban renewal project, and the sculptures now reside in the Grand Rapids Public Museum. Two other

°Here and hereafter indicates that the sculpture under discussion is not illustrated.

buildings erected by women's groups during this period carry terra cotta reliefs on the facade. A dolphin motif, also found on two other Grand Rapids buildings of 1884, can be found on the Ladies Literary Club (1887) [p. 59]. Elegant cartouches, filled with musical instruments and flanked by cupids, decorate the St. Cecilia Music Society Building (c. 1894) [p. 63].

Civic improvement was also reflected in the appearance of practical items like cast iron clocks and fountains. Several of the city parks, including Fulton Street and Crescent parks, used to have fountains similar to the one located at the former Soldiers' Home (c. 1893) [p. 85].

Another civic improvement was the development of cemeteries which also served as public parks. This type of rural cemetery had been developed in the East around the time that settlers began to move into Michigan. Oak Hill Cemetery is among the several picturesque cemetery-parks which were laid out in Grand Rapids. The north side was dedicated on October 25, 1859, while the south side, originally called Valley City Cemetery, was dedicated on December 17, 1860. The beautiful settings, considered works of art in themselves, stimulated the creation of larger and more elaborate monuments to impress, inspire, and charm the visitors. Albert Baxter speaks thus of the Grand Rapids cemeteries in 1891.

> ...They contain many illustrations of the growth by culture of the taste of the people, in the matter of their improvement and adornment. Therein are a great many samples of artistic conception and skill shown in the chiseled marble, and of the manifestations of affection in family circles exhibited in shrubbery and floral decorations about the resting places of their loved ones departed (p. 441).

There are a number of interesting monuments and mausoleums in Oak Hill Cemetery, including Otto Vanselow's extraordinary *Kendall Monument* (1900) [p. 114] and the Egyptian mausoleum for A. B. Watson (1914) [p. 112].

Communities also found the time and money to memorialize their heroes. Statues of soldiers, politicians, poets, and civic leaders were erected to serve a dual purpose. They honored the past, and they were morally uplifting to present and future generations. In addition to the previously mentioned *John Ball Memorial,* other monuments which honor those who shaped Grand Rapids include Lorado Taft's *Thomas D. Gilbert* (1895) [p. 43]; the sundial erected in memory of Moses V. Aldrich (c. 1925) [p. 98]; and Horace Colby's *Captain Charles E. Belknap* (1913) [p. 79]. When the Gilbert bust was dedicated on June 5, 1896, several eloquent speeches were delivered on the civic virtues of Gilbert and on monuments. Typical of the sentiments expressed are those by Colonel G. G. Briggs who said:

> In the erection of this memorial to our departed friend, we but follow the example of a time-honored custom. The civilized nations of the earth have ever considered it a sacred duty to raise statues and memorial monuments to their benefactors, and thus perpetuate the memory of their honored dead. These memorials are object lessons speaking to succeeding generations of lives and deeds worthy of emulation. Republics may be ungrateful, but the great heart of our common humanity has ever a place for its benefactors, and in the future, as in the past, the memory of such will be preserved and honored (*Grand Rapids Democrat,* June 6, 1896:8).

Gilbert's bust is appropriately placed in what was then known as Fulton Street Park, renamed Veterans Memorial Park in 1956. Originally the county courthouse square, Gilbert lovingly tended the park which served as a major focal point for the city until the completion in 1969 of Calder Plaza in Vandenburg Center. The bust of Gilbert is paired with William Couper's bust of Henry W. Longfellow (1912) [p. 45]. The Longfellow bust and Adolph Weinman's bust of Abraham Lincoln (c. 1913) [p. 67], which is located in nearby Lincoln Place, were gifts of that remarkable Grand Rapids woman Loraine Pratt Immen.

Like the Lincoln statue, many memorials were not erected until long after the death of the person or event they commemorated. The Gilbert bust, however, was erected within a year of Gilbert's death. When the bust was formally presented by Colonel Briggs to the city, Mayor L. C. Snow promised that the grateful people of Grand Rapids would "guard this monument with sacred care." In spite of his promise, the Gilbert bust and other memorials go unnoticed today. They remain a testimonial to the fervent patriotism of their time. The war memorials also reflect the belief that wars were waged for humanitarian reasons.

Hardly a city is without its war memorial, and Grand Rapids lays claim to several. The above-mentioned Lincoln bust is a memorial to the man and to the Civil War. One of Grand Rapids' earliest war memorials is Leon Coquard's embattled *Soldiers' Monument* (c. 1885) [p. 56]. These two memorials and the *Soldiers' Monument* located in the cemetery of the old Soldiers' Home (c. 1893) [p. 87] reflect the strong antislavery sentiment in Michigan during the Civil War. The later popular Spanish American War is memorialized in Theodore Alice Ruggles Kitson's *The Hiker* (c. 1927) [p. 68].

The decline of the war memorial and memorials in general began in the United States after the disillusionment of World War I, despite our victory. Contributing to this decline was a preference for memorials in the form of parks or buildings rather than sculpture. This was nearly the case with Ralph Demmon's *Memorial Pillars* (1926) [p. 41] which won out over a proposed memorial building. Other World War I memorials include the Celtic Cross, St. Mark's Episcopal Church (1921)° and the *Polish War Memorial*, Holy Cross Cemetery (1929)°. Located in Creston is the *World War II Memorial* (1942)°. After Fulton Street Park was changed to Veteran's Memorial Park in 1956, two additional memorials were added to the *Memorial Pillars*. The first stelae (1957), carved by F. C. Ruppel and S. J. Terhaar, commemorate those who died in World War II and the Korean War, while the later stelae (1975) memorialize those who served in the Vietnam War [p. 41]. The name change and the placement of five memorials in the public park, which served for so long as the center of the city, is mute testimony to the belief in the civic virtue of monuments. For the most part, the more recent war memorials in Grand Rapids have been left to the monument carver. Since the Vietnamese Conflict, antiwar sentiment in the United States has sometimes led to the destruction of past monuments and to the creation of protest monuments.

The period between the Civil War and World War I was indeed the golden age of the commemorative monument. Sculptor and citizen alike felt the need to express American ideals in equally lofty styles. The classical Beaux-Arts style, so-called because its source was the École des Beaux-Arts (National Academy of Fine Arts) in Paris, became an "official" style for American ideals. The Beaux-Arts style reached its sumptuous apogee at the Chicago Worlds Columbian Exposition of 1893 and lingered on into the 1930s.

One of the aspects of the Beaux-Arts and other styles that were popular before and after the turn of the century is the decorative element. Nineteenth-century examples have already been cited which employed terra cotta in the decoration of buildings. The extensive use of decorative terra cotta, perhaps because of the proximity to Chicago, continued on into the twentieth century. Among extant examples are the lions and other reliefs on the Heystek Building (c. 1912) [p. 37]; reliefs from the Metz Building (c. 1912) [p. 63] now preserved on the Saint Cecilia Society Music Building; Corrado Joseph Parducci's Indian and other reliefs on the Michigan National Bank (1926); and the lovely peacocks on the Williard Building (1930) [p. 60]. High cost and the preference for streamlined modern architecture sounded the death knell for decorative terra cotta during the depression.

The seminal modern art movement had already begun to challenge the flourishing Beaux-Arts school at the beginning of the twentieth century. Artists began to carve directly in wood and stone. Since they responded to the natural forms of the material, their works tended toward abstraction. The stone carver was thus eliminated and works became smaller and more intimate. A new class of patrons was beginning to develop which could afford sculpture for private settings, though their tastes continued to embrace traditional styles rather than modern art. The popularity of garden sculpture is reflected in the above-mentioned sundial and the lions and urns at the old Lowe Estate (c. 1910) [p. 111] which is now a part of Aquinas College.

Between World War I and World War II, a new style developed which was more in keeping with the twentieth century. Once again, the style originated in Paris and was called Art Moderne or Art Deco after the 1925 Exhibition of Decorative and Industrial Arts. This crisp, geometric style created a streamlined yet bold effect which is reflected in the reliefs on the Rest Lawn Mausoleum (1932) [p. 116]. A growing interest in mausoleum burial prompted the construction of this second facility after the completion of the earlier Graceland Mausoleum (c. 1923) [p. 127], which is also articulated with sculpture. A softer Art Deco can be found in Corrado Joseph Parducci's reliefs located on the Civic Center (1932) [p. 31]. Art Deco, particularly as a figurative style, continued on through the 1950s in a progressively bland manner. These super-muscled heroes represented American ideals until an abstract vocabularly received public support and acceptance in the 1960s.

The 1930s depression provided an impetus for the proliferation of these bulky, angular figures. During this period of social concern, there was an inward turning and an emphasis on the individual worker. The United States government emerged as a patron of the arts through programs like the Works Progress Administration (WPA), Federal Art Project. Initiated in 1935, the name of the program was changed to the Work Projects Administration in 1939 and was terminated in 1942. While Parducci's reliefs reflect the figurative style of the 1930s, they were created as part of a Grand Rapids relief project under the leadership of City Manager George W. Welsh and were not a WPA project. Parducci recently remarked that he was required to live in Grand Rapids while he modeled the reliefs for the Civic Center (he stayed at the YMCA) and was the only employee to be paid in cash (all other workers were paid in Grand Rapids scrip). For the most part, it appears that Grand Rapids did not participate in any WPA sculptural projects. In fact, from the depression onward, there was very little sculpture activity in Grand Rapids until the late 1960s.

It was not until after World War II that modern sculpture began to blossom, even though the seeds had been sown and cultivated throughout the first half of the twentieth century. Traditional form (often the human form) and space were in the process of transformation through new materials, techniques, and thought. Representational forms were abstracted into organic and geometric forms. The relationship of space to a solid mass was altered by incorporating space within the form. As pedestals began to disappear, space was increasingly extended and the viewer was increasingly involved with the work. Such spatial transformations have paved the way for today's large-scale works which embrace a total environment. Such a work is Robert Morris' *Grand Rapids Project* (1974) [p. 80].

The application of industrial materials and techniques, including steel, plastic, and welding, allowed sculpture to be constructed rather than modeled or carved. Sculpture could incorporate found objects or have moveable parts. Sculptors were no longer bound to express heroic American ideals in their work but were free to explore sculpture as an individual expression. Today, the subject of sculpture may be form, materials, process, or something as ephemeral as a concept or performance. The dimensions of sculpture can be stretched even further if one includes permanent works like photographs or video tapes which document ephemeral art. A recent work, which now remains primarily in memory or documents, is Otto Piene's *Grand Rapids Carousel* (1979)°. This sky sculpture, flown over Festival '79, was commissioned by the Women's Committee of the Grand Rapids Art Museum in conjunction with their exhibition *5 Artists/5 Technologies.*

During the 1960s urban renewal programs were initiated across the United States in an attempt to revitalize decaying inner cities. In Grand Rapids old structures were razed to make way for the Vandenburg Center. Plans for the Center called for a fountain, but citizen involvement later altered the plans to include Grand Rapids first abstract work, Alexander Calder's *La Grande Vitesse* (1969) [p. 19]. This work, the first to be funded in the United States by the National Endowment for the Arts, has set the pace for the considerable sculptural activity which Grand Rapids has experienced in the 1970s.

Once again the government has become a patron of the arts through programs like urban renewal, the National Endowment for the Arts, the General Services Art-in-Architecture Program, and the Michigan Council for the Arts. Among other works which have received funding through the National Endowment for the Arts are Morris' earthwork mentioned above; Joseph Kinnebrew's *Grand River Sculpture and Fish Ladder* (1975) [p. 75]; and Ronald Watson's *Solar Painting: the Terminator* (1975) [p. 25]. Mark di Suvero's *Motu,* also mentioned above, was commissioned through the General Services Art-in-Architecture Program.

In addition to the catalytic Calder and government support, sculpture has also received an impetus from Festival, the Women's Committee of the Grand Rapids Art Museum, and Urban Concerns, Inc. Most important, all of the sculptural activity has taken place in conjunction with city officials who have capitalized on their Calder by including the image on letterhead, street signs, and garbage trucks.

Festival is the annual art celebration which began on Calder Plaza the year after *La Grand Vitesse* was installed. To date Festival has purchased playground sculpture which is permanently located in city parks at the conclusion of each year's celebration. The pieces include Thomas Leech's untitled works located in John Ball Memorial Park (1973)°; Mary Preminger's *Recreform* (1974) [p. 105]; Joseph Kinnebrew's *Kid Katwalk* (1975) [p. 77]; Hy Zelkowitz's *Lorrie's Button* (1976) [p. 29]; Robbin Crawford's *Orange-Ganic Domino* (1977) [p. 103]; Robin Jensen's *Earth Loops* (1978) [p. 101]; and James Kuiper's *Split* (1979) [p. 119].

The Calder brought national recognition to Grand Rapids, as did the 1973 exhibition *Sculpture Off the Pedestal.* Included in the show were drawings for Morris' earthwork which was realized the following year. The exhibition, earthwork and sky sculpture were sponsored by the dynamic Women's Committee of the Grand Rapids Art Museum.

Another effective group is Urban Concerns, Inc., which has been responsible for enriching the city with several art projects. Sculpture which has been placed in Grand Rapids through this group includes Loretta Stephenson's untitled work (1972) [p. 33]; Nathan Horowitz's *Vesta* (1973) [p. 22]; Thomas Leech's *Sizby* (1973) [p. 47]; Barbara Uhl's untitled work (1975) [p. 51]; and Watson's *Solar Painting: the Terminator.*

With the advent of the Calder, sculpture and sculptural sites are once again serving as a means of identification for those who live in Grand Rapids, just as they did in an earlier era. The earlier strong leadership, which brought about sculpture and which was also commemorated by sculpture, is in evidence again on both the public and private level. While leadership was and is to a certain extent elitist, the impact, however controversial, is not.

Grand Rapids, once known as the "Furniture City," is known today for its sculpture. The earlier furniture industry, however, has not been forgotten. Terra cotta reliefs depicting the tools of the trade can be found on the exterior of the present day Exhibitors Building (c. 1925)°.

This building was remodeled in 1925 to house showrooms for the furniture industry and renamed the Fine Arts Building. Two previously mentioned works also serve as reminders of the past industry. They are Winter's *Legend of Grand Rapids* which portrays a vignette of the industry and the city's most recent sculpture, Kuiper's *Split,* which uses wood in remembrance of furniture manufacturing in Grand Rapids.

What the 80s will hold for Grand Rapids is, of course, anybody's guess. But, given the sculptural activities of the 70s, the next decade could be even more exciting.

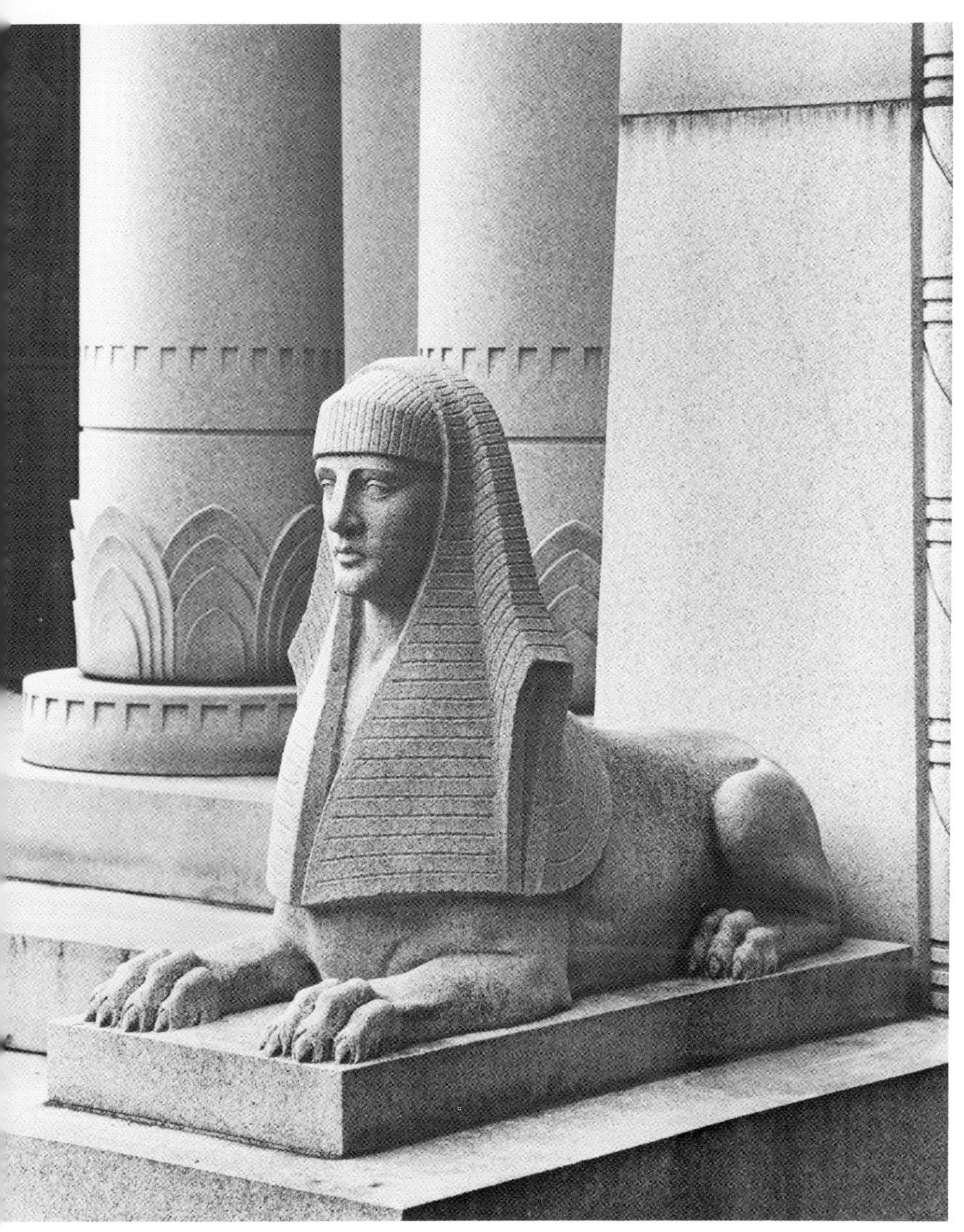

Detail, Watson mausoleum, Oak Hill Cemetery (E-3, p. 112).

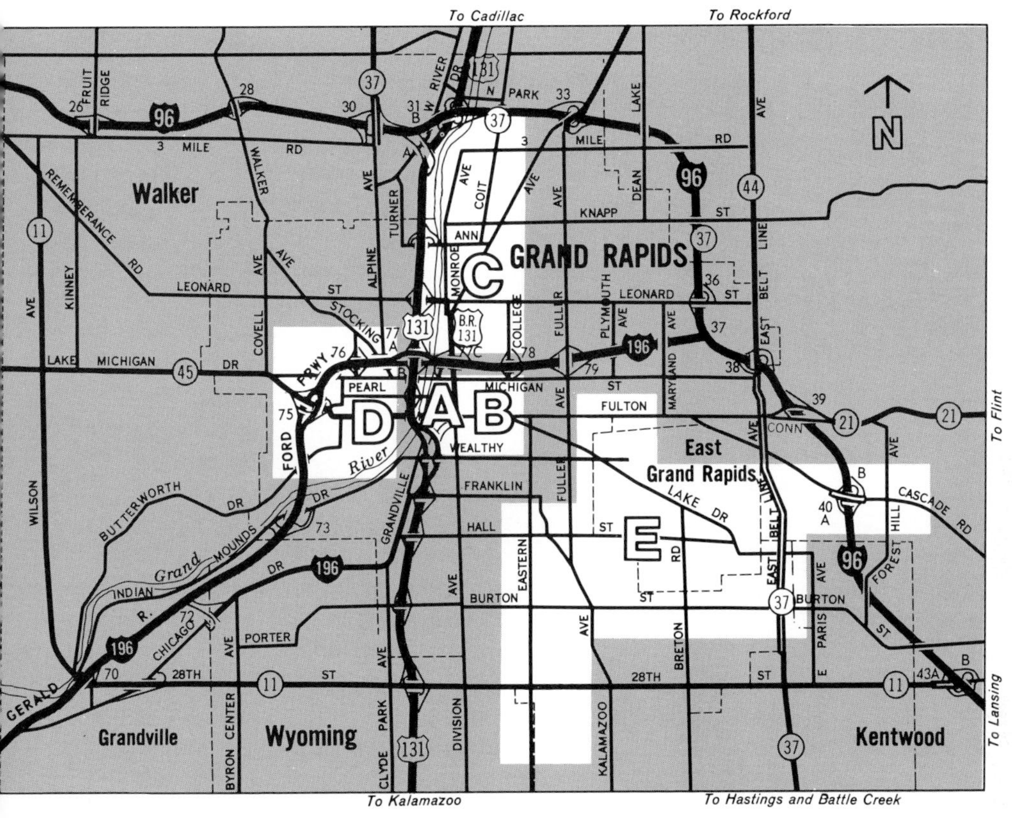

OUTDOOR SCULPTURE BY GEOGRAPHIC AREAS

A. CALDER PLAZA

B. VETERANS MEMORIAL PARK

C. NORTH

D. WEST

E. SOUTHEAST

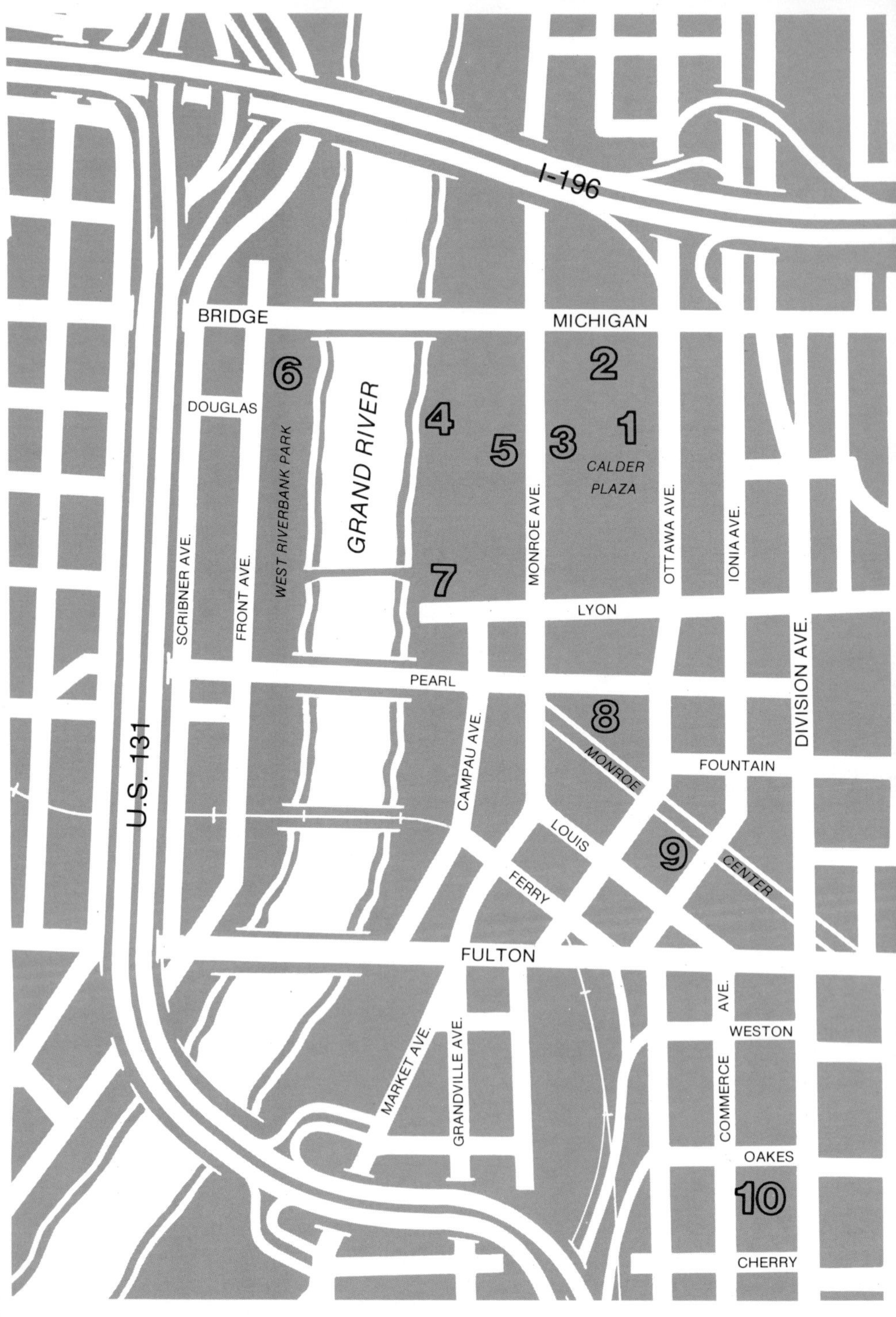

I-196
BRIDGE
MICHIGAN
DOUGLAS
GRAND RIVER
WEST RIVERBANK PARK
CALDER PLAZA
SCRIBNER AVE.
FRONT AVE.
MONROE AVE.
OTTAWA AVE.
IONIA AVE.
LYON
PEARL
DIVISION AVE.
CAMPAU AVE.
MONROE
FOUNTAIN
U.S. 131
LOUIS
FERRY
CENTER
FULTON
WESTON
COMMERCE AVE.
MARKET AVE.
GRANDVILLE AVE.
OAKES
CHERRY
1
2
3
4
5
6
7
8
9
10

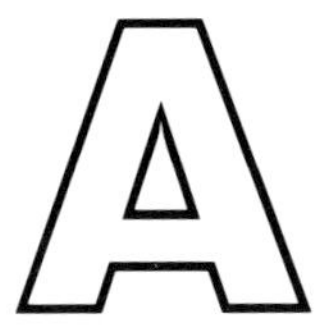

CALDER PLAZA AREA

1. Alexander Calder, LA GRANDE VITESSE
   Calder Plaza

2. Mark di Suvero, MOTU
   Calder Plaza

3. Nathan Horowitz, VESTA
   Calder Plaza

4. Ronald Watson, SOLAR PAINTING: THE TERMINATOR
   Justice Park

5. Joseph E. Kinnebrew IV, HERE MAN'S DESIRE...("JUSTICE")
   Hall of Justice

6. Hy Zelkowitz, LORRIE'S BUTTON
   West Riverbank Park

7. Corrado Joseph Parducci, CIVIC AUDITORIUM RELIEFS

8. Loretta Stephenson, UNTITLED
   Sears Mini-Park

9. Corrado Joseph Parducci, MICHIGAN NATIONAL BANK RELIEFS

10. Artist Unknown, LIONS
    Heystek Building

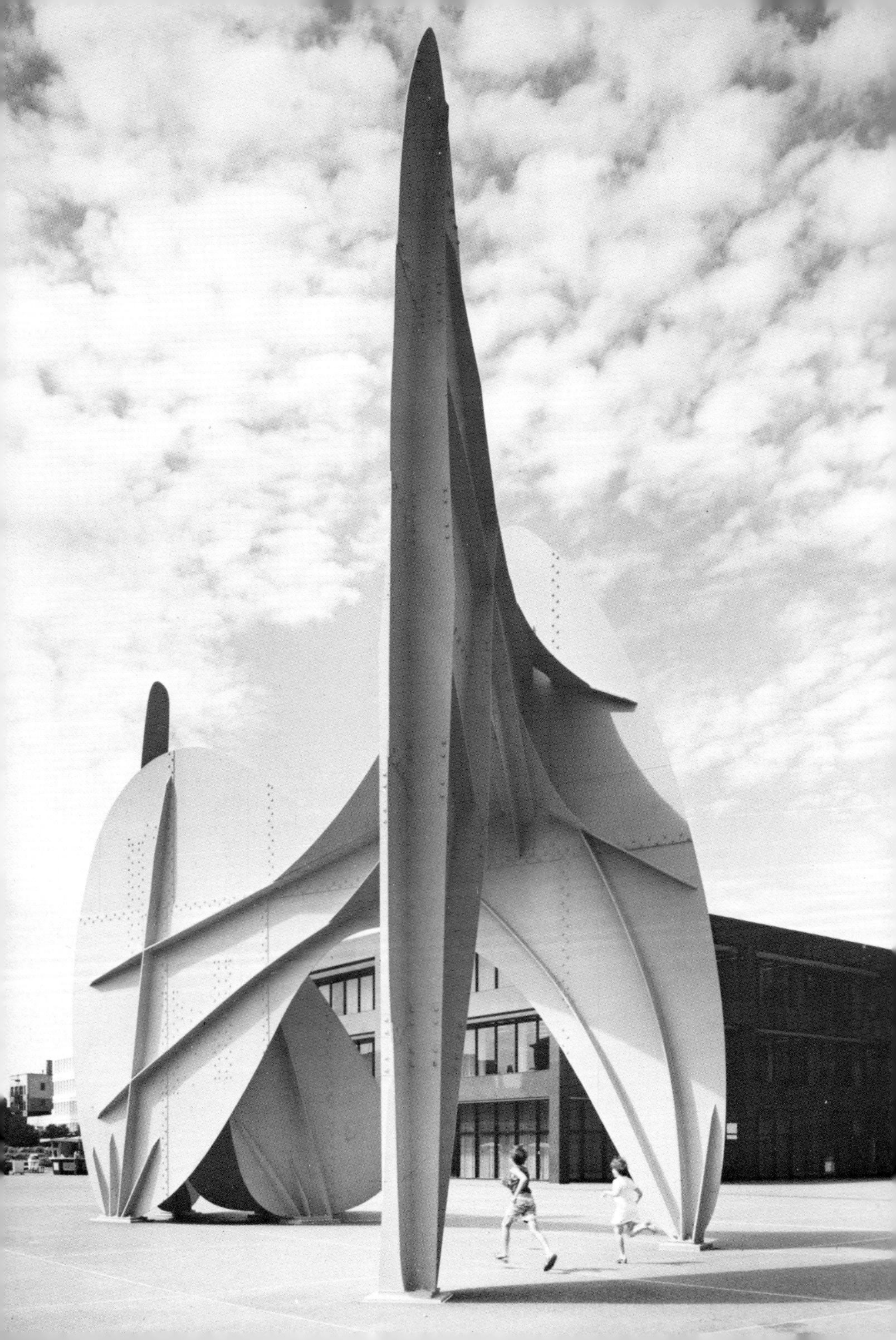

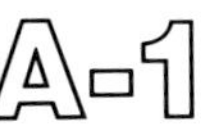

Alexander Calder (1898-1976)

LA GRANDE VITESSE

1969, steel, 43′
[CA 69]

Calder Plaza, Vandenberg Center
Ottawa N.W. between Michigan and Lyon, Grand Rapids

Vandenberg Center, an Urban Renewal Project, originally included a fountain for the plaza. When Henry Geldzahler from the Metropolitan Museum in New York visited Grand Rapids in 1967, he suggested that the city apply for funds to place a sculpture on the plaza and *La Grande Vitesse* became the first sculpture to be funded by the National Endowment for the Arts through their Works of Art in Public Places. Matching funds were provided through local private sources and the sculpture was dedicated on June 14, 1969. The joyous undulating forms of this stabile, whose title translates into the great swiftness or grand rapids, suggests the surging motion of rapids and of life. The Calder, as it is commonly referred to, serves not only as a counterpoint to the modern Skidmore, Owings, and Merrill city and county buildings, but as a big red catalyst to many arts related activities, including the debut of Festival on Calder Plaza in 1970 and the Calder design painted on the roof of the county building in 1974. Images of the sculpture can be found on city letterhead, garbage trucks, and street signs.

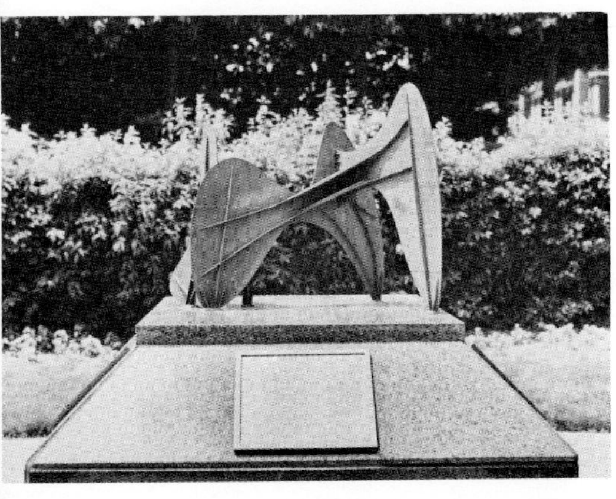

A scale model for the sightless, fashioned by Hetzer Harsock with monies provided by the Keeler Fund, was placed on the plaza in 1976.

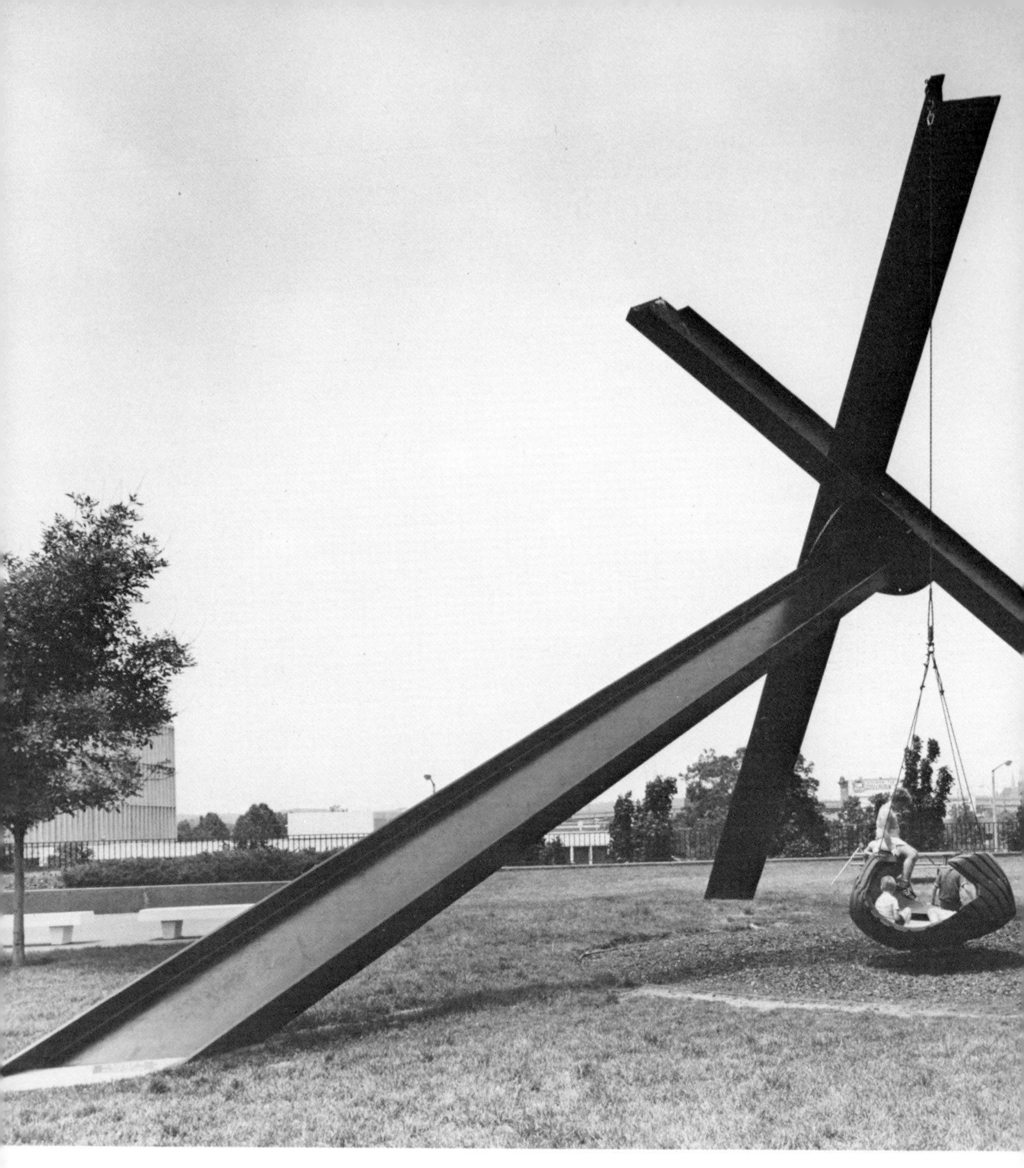

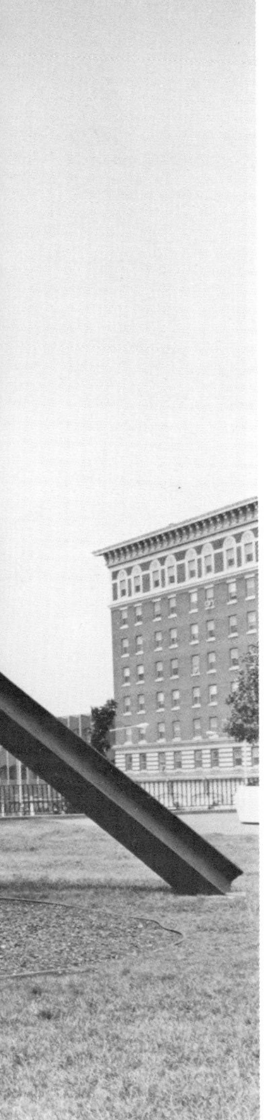

A-2

Mark di Suvero (1933-   )

MOTU

1977, cor-ten steel and rubber tire, 35′

Gerald R. Ford Federal Building and U.S. Courthouse
Calder Plaza, Vandenberg Center
Ottawa N.W. between Michigan and Lyon, Grand Rapids

In 1973, Mark di Suvero exhibited *Are Years What? (For Marianne Moore)* (1967) in this same site for the exhibition *Sculpture Off the Pedestal.* He was subsequently commissioned by the General Services Administration through their Art-in-Architecture Program to create a permanent work to enhance the Federal Building which was designed by Kingscott Associates of Kalamazoo, Michigan. When the sculpture was completed, the GSA would not accept the work because it did not correspond to the original model. Di Suvero found it necessary to alter the model after he came to Grand Rapids to construct the piece. Factors which brought about these changes included wind velocity, weight, and a greater familiarity with the site and the people of Grand Rapids. The GSA reversed their decision after a vigorous campaign was waged by supporters from the Grand Rapids community. The sculpture, dedicated on June 3 during Festival '77, takes its title from the city motto, *Motu Viget,* which is freely translated "strength through activity." This strong, linear work, which encompasses an open triangular space, is constructed of three beams which pierce and interlock with each other. The viewer is invited to climb the thrusting beams (though a sign warns that this is dangerous) or swing in the suspended rubber gondola.

Nathan Horowitz (1947-)

VESTA

1973, cor-ten steel and steel, 35′
[NH 10-73]

County Building
Calder Plaza, Vandenberg Center
Ottawa N.W. between Michigan and Lyon, Grand Rapids

Vesta, created for the stairwell behind the County Building, was a gift from the artist and Urban Concerns, Inc. This sculpture is the last in a series that deals with planar penetration. The first two works are titled *Chastity* and *Purity* and are located in suburban Detroit. In this particular work, two beams pierce a flat plane. One of these beams thrusts its way up through the stairwell, thus involving the viewer as he moves up and down the stairs. The title, *Vesta,* refers to the Roman goddess of the hearth whose temple was kept by vestal virgins. This sculpture, however, is a reverse image of the chaste Vesta.

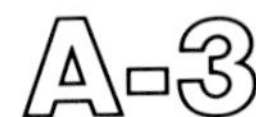

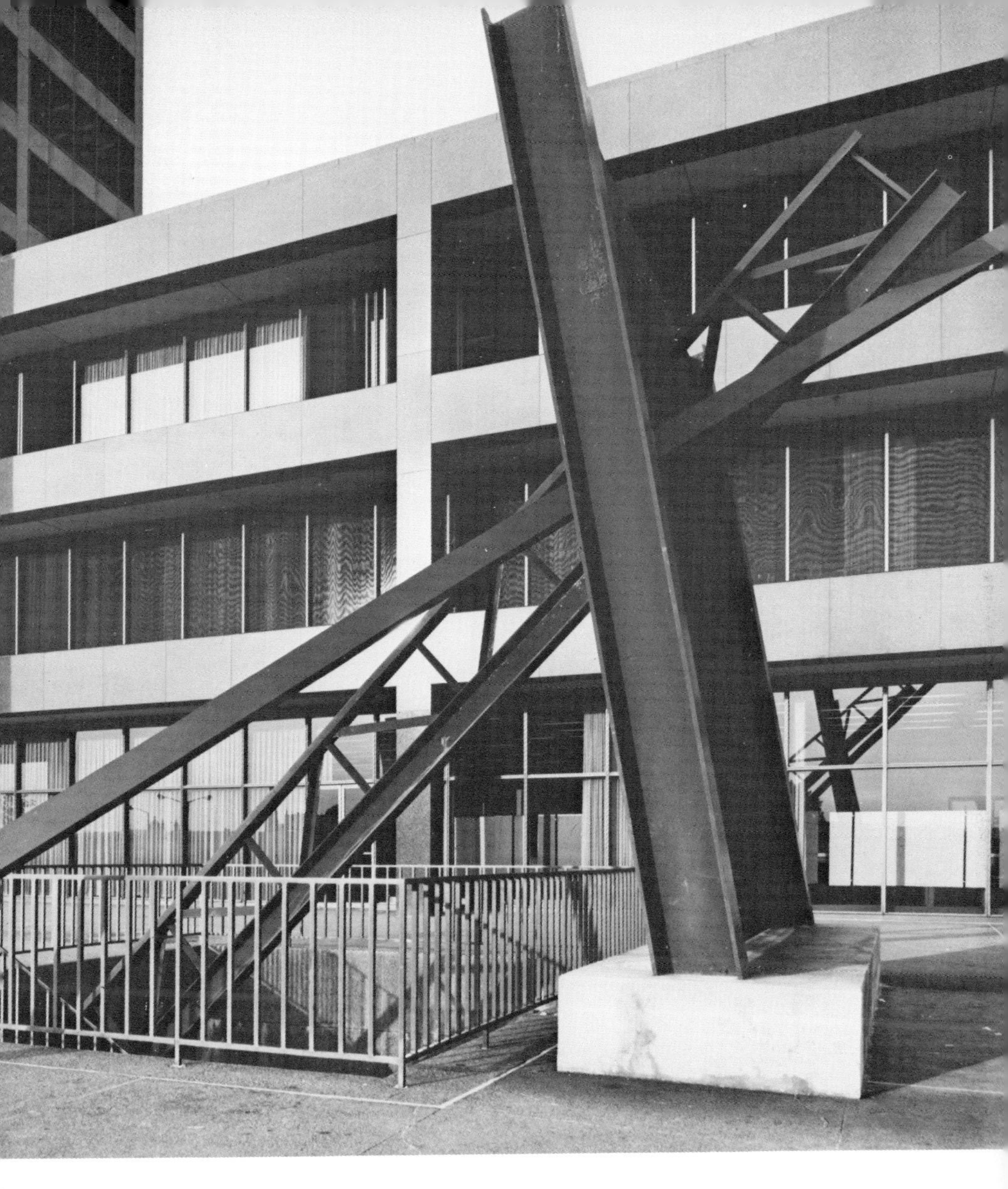

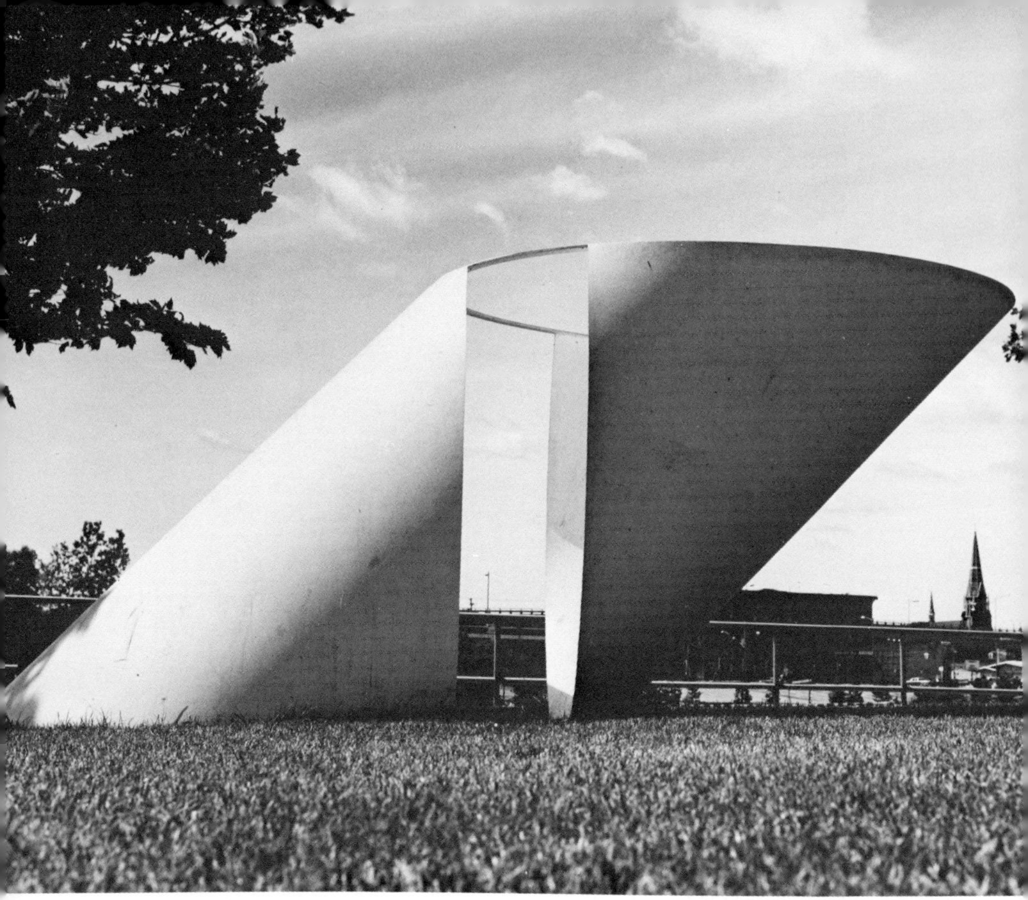

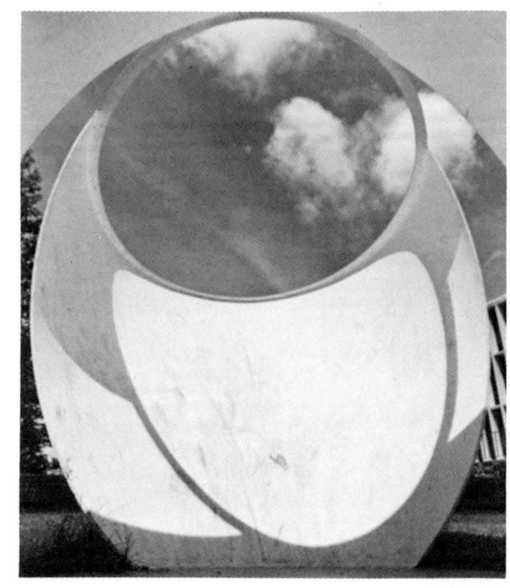

View from inside
the sculpture.

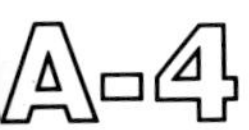

Ronald Watson (1941-   )

SOLAR PAINTING: THE TERMINATOR

1975, steel, 6′

Justice Park
Monroe N.W. between Michigan and Lyon, Grand Rapids

Solar Painting: The Terminator was created in 1975 for the Chicago invitational exhibition *Sculpture for a New Era.* It evolved out of experiments with aluminized defraction grading which reflects the color spectrum and projects it onto adjacent surfaces. For practical and aesthetic reasons, the inner aluminized surfaces were replaced with white paint. The title, which includes the word terminator, space terminology for the juncture of light and shadow on a planet's surface, describes the visual phenomena of ever-changing patterns painted by the sun. Experientially, one may also walk though the split cylinder. The sculpture which became the focal point of Justice Park in 1978, was made possible through the artist, Urban Concerns, Inc., the Women's Committee of the Grand Rapids Art Museum, the Michigan Council for the Arts, and the National Endowment for the Arts. Watson's piece bespeaks his efforts, along with others, to reclaim the riverbanks for an urban population.

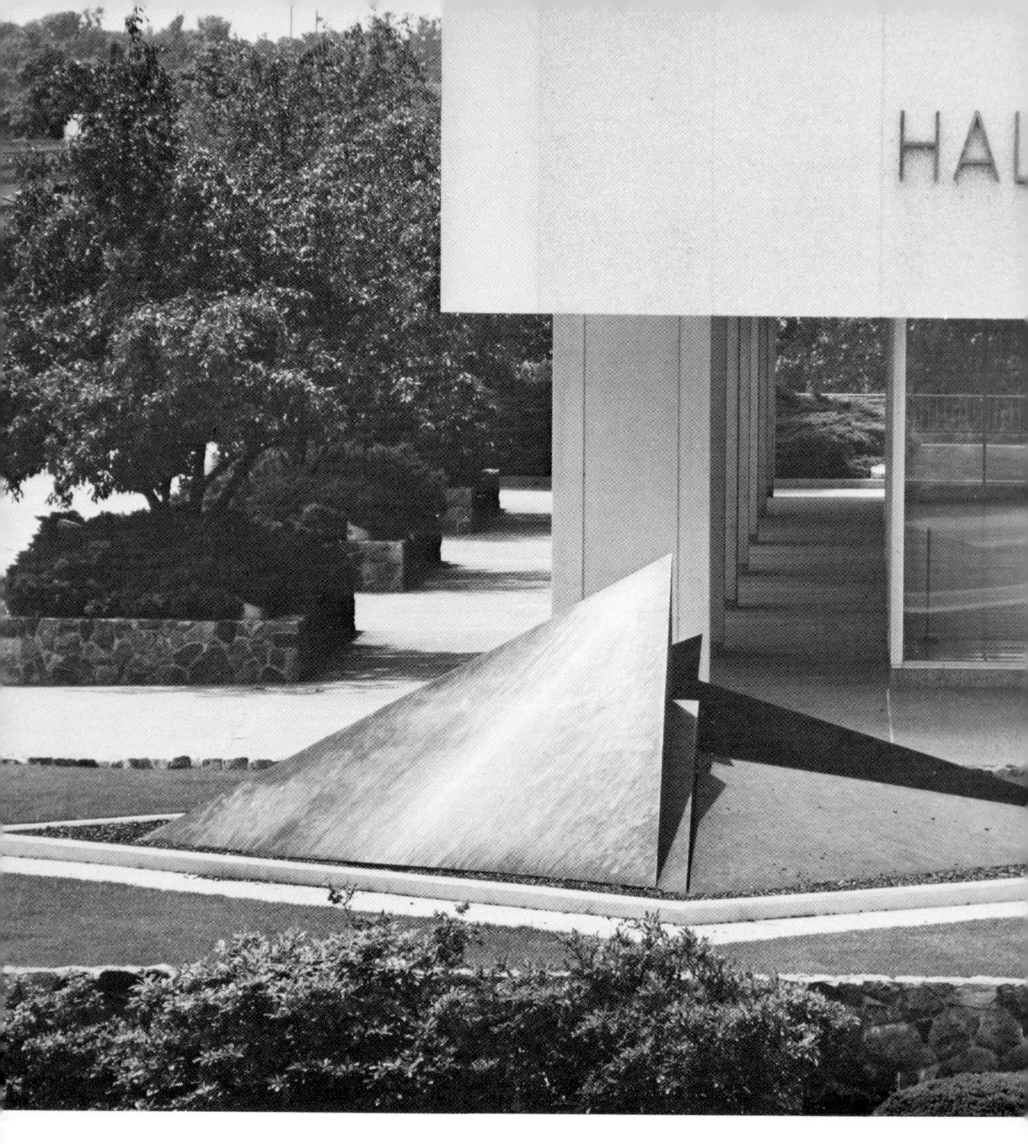
HAL

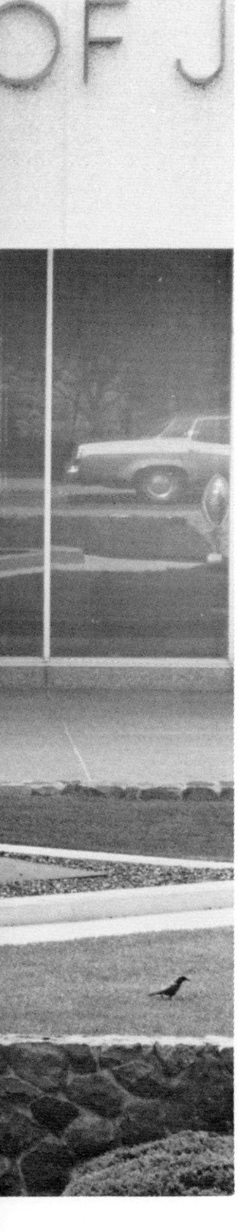

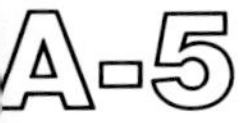

Joseph E. Kinnebrew IV (1942-)

HERE MAN'S DESIRE IS FOR PERFECT AND PREDICTABLE JUSTICE. TOWARDS THAT END HE MAKES LAWS TO ESTABLISH AND MAINTAIN IMPERFECT AND UNPREDICTABLE MAN IN A SOCIETY WHICH ONLY OCCASIONALLY UNDERSTANDS ITS HUMAN ESSENCE AND ALMOST NEVER SEES OR EVIDENCES THE CONCEPT OF TRUE JUSTICE. WE MUST UNDERSTAND THAT JUSTICE IS A HUMAN INVENTION AND POTENTIALLY ONE OF THE GREATEST TESTIMONIES TO OUR EXCELLENCE. IF WE FAIL TO ATTAIN THE MAJESTY OF JUSTICE THE PRICE WILL BE SIMPLE AND ETERNAL. THE COSMOS WILL FORGET US. ("Justice")

1977, myari r steel, 7′

[see title. Kinnebrew IV May 17, 1978]

Hall of Justice
333 Monroe N.W., Grand Rapids

"Justice" was commissioned by friends of Richard L. Spindle, a Grand Rapids attorney who died in an automobile accident on July 10, 1975. The pyramid has long been associated with funerary monuments, justice, and wisdom. This low, somber, and fragmented pyramidal form, appropriately located outside the Hall of Justice, is positioned one degree east of north reflecting the artist's interest in myths and fables. The title, a personal statement of justice, is stamped into the metal and will disappear in a few years.

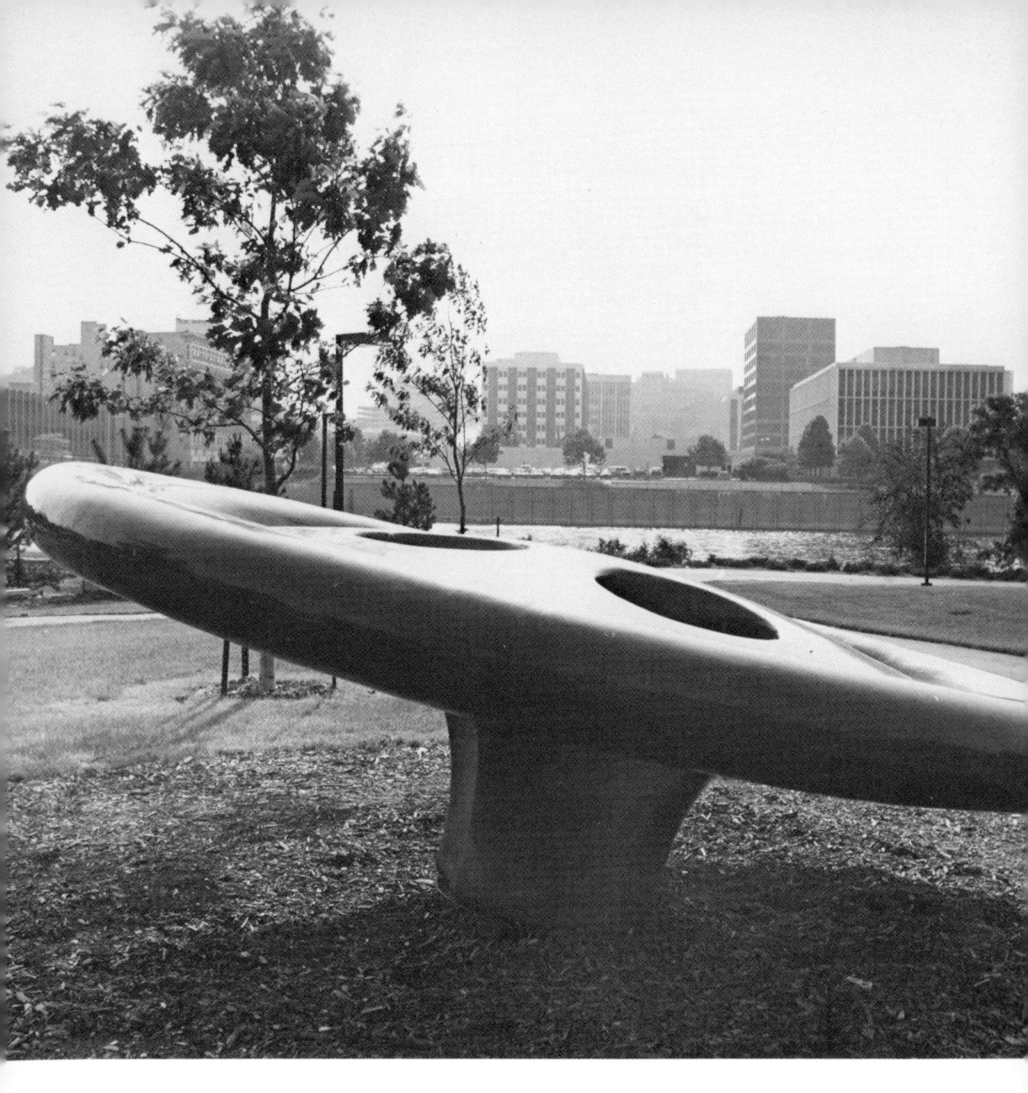

Hy Zelkowitz (1946-   )

LORRIE'S BUTTON

1976, fiberglass and urethane foam, 4′

[HZ 76]

West Riverbank Park
Front N.W. between Michigan and Pearl, Grand Rapids

The large-scale red button was winner of the Playground Sculpture Design Competition for Festival '76. The button was temporarily placed on Calder Plaza and moved to its final destination across the river in time for the dedication of West Riverbank Park on October 25, 1978. Since the park was a Bicentennial project and since *Lorrie's Button* was created during the Bicentennial year, Hy Zelkowitz chose this form to tie the past to the future through the continuum of children. Named for a friend's child, "the button is symbolic of the children of America joining the earth, our past, to the top layer of growth, the grass, our future." Children are invited to climb on the button and through the holes, slide on its surface, and play underneath in the buttonhole. The button was originally part of a proposal to link downtown Grand Rapids together with six buttons and buttonholes. The button and the park are part of a continuing effort to focus on the river as a means of joining together, rather than dividing, the city of Grand Rapids.

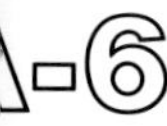

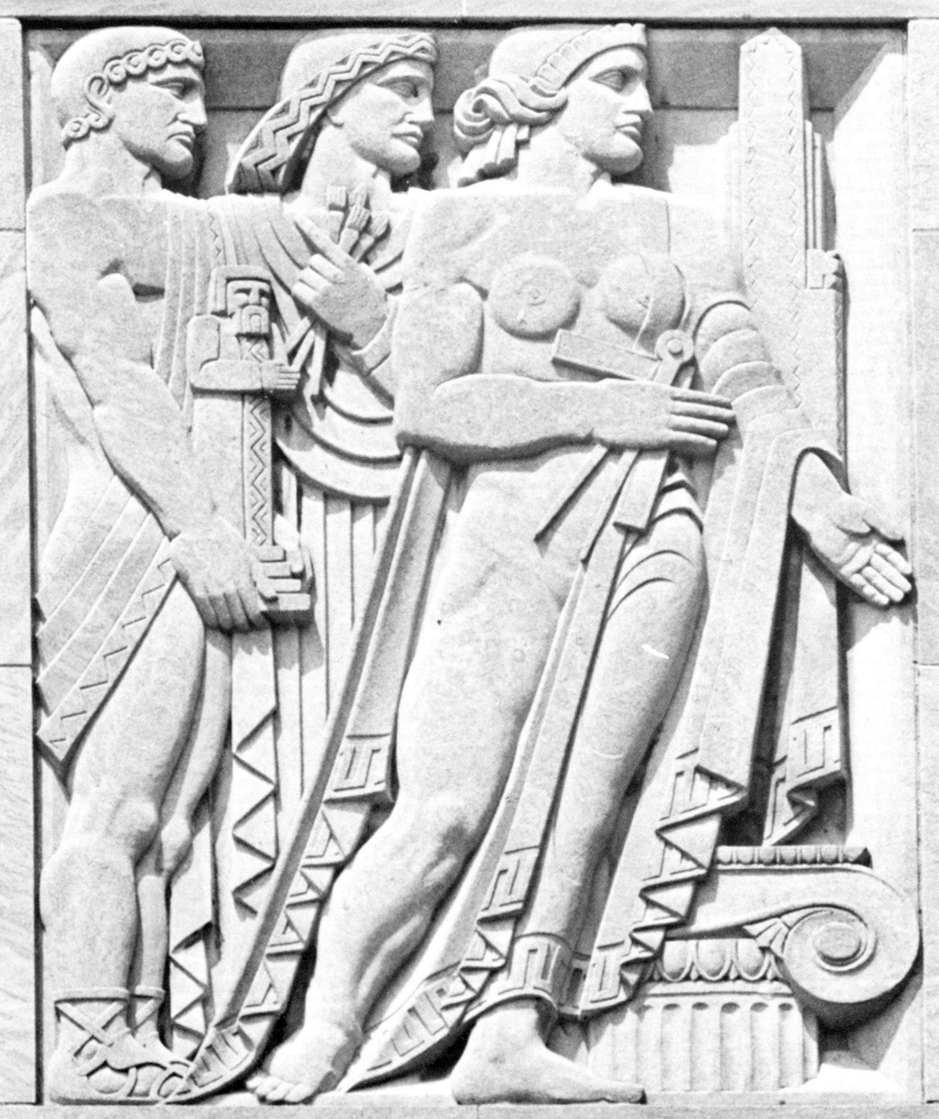
FINE ARTS

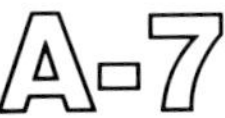

Corrado Joseph Parducci (1900-)

CIVIC AUDITORIUM RELIEFS

1932, limestone, FINE ARTS 6'10"

George W. Welsh Civic Auditorium (Civic Auditorium)
227 Lyon N.W., Grand Rapids

On January 2, 1933, dedication ceremonies were held in the new Art Deco Civic Auditorium which was designed by the Grand Rapids firm of Robinson and Campau, with Smith, Hinchman and Grylls of Detroit as associate architects. The building was built under the aegis of City Manager George W. Welsh, for whom the building was renamed in 1975, and provided space for cultural, civic, and convention activities. It was also a city relief project which provided employment for Grand Rapids citizens during the depression. The classically oriented sculptural decoration is executed in a broad thirties style. It includes the shell and wave motif along the roofline, signs of the zodiac, city and state seals, and allegorical figures which represent Sports, Industry, Electricity, Sculpture, Textiles, Printing, Drama, Fine Arts, Music, Philosophy, Commerce, and Science.

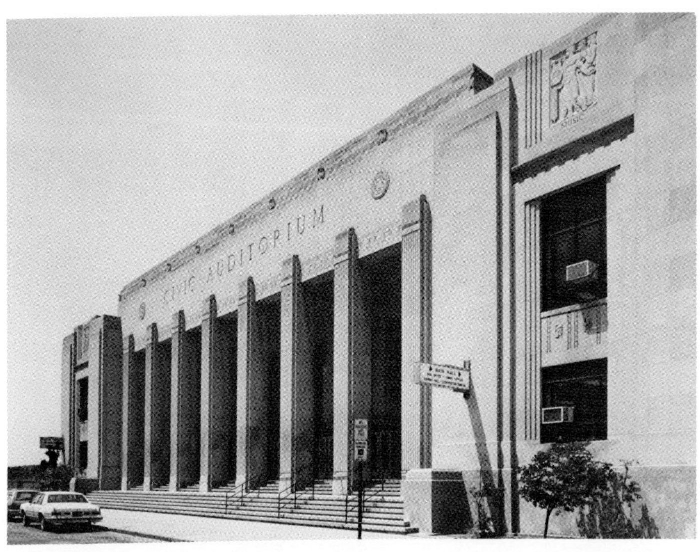

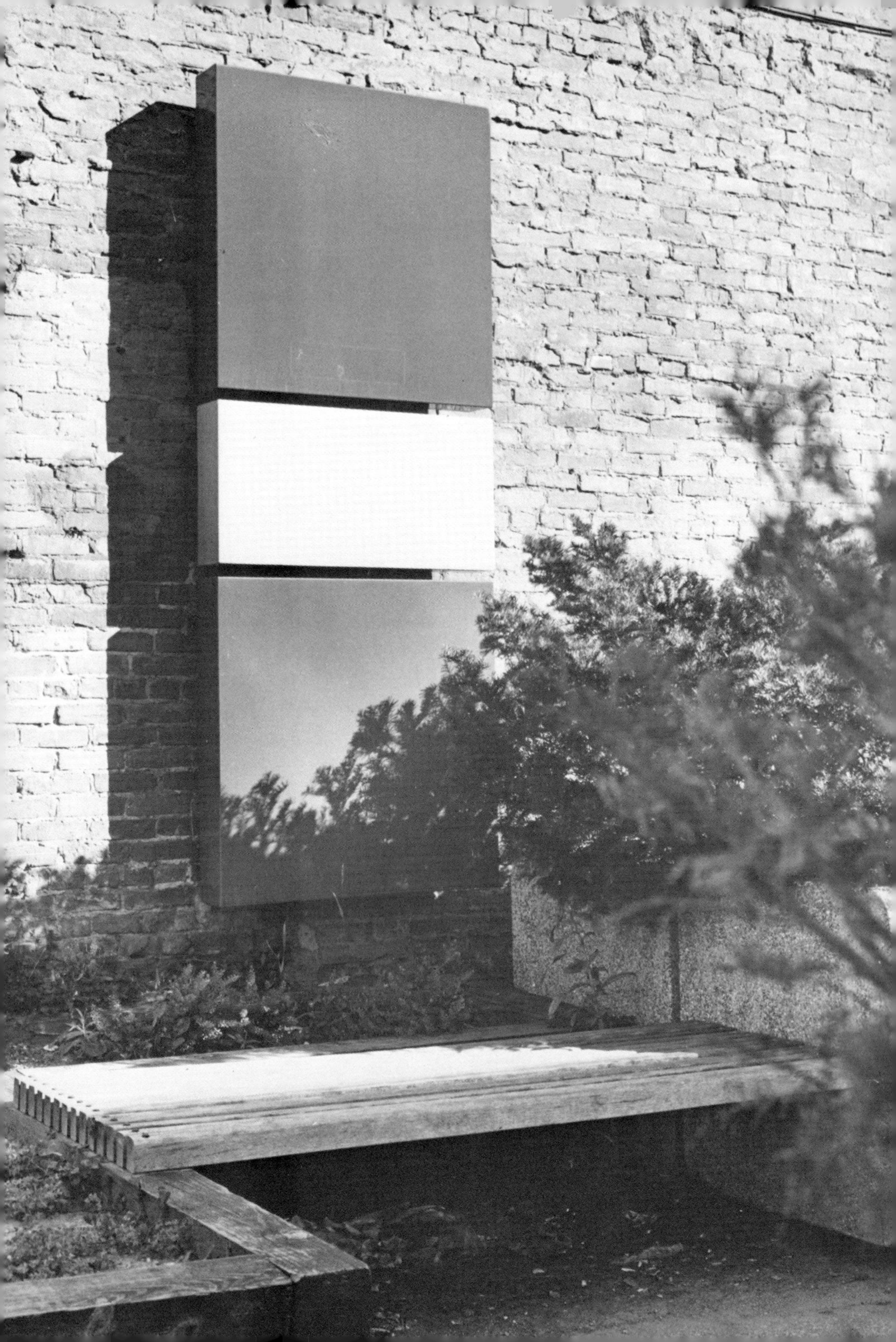

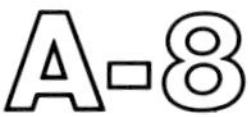

Loretta Stephenson (1938-   )

UNTITLED

1972, enameled steel, 7′8″

Sears Mini-Park
Monroe Center, Pearl and Ottawa Streets N.W., Grand Rapids

Urban Concerns, Inc., provided the stimulus for the development of a small urban park which was designed by Grand Rapids architect Robert E. Hicks (1930-   ). The park was designed as a quiet oasis with a work of art and interlocking benches and planters for trees. The focal point of the park is Stephenson's smooth, minimal sculpture which hangs from the textured brick wall like a painting. The work, which appears to float on the wall, is composed of two rhythmical blue rectangles which are punctuated by a narrower yellow form. The use of primary colors reinforces the primary forms. The mini-park project was made possible through the efforts of Hicks and Stephenson, who donated their time, and through funds raised by Urban Concerns.

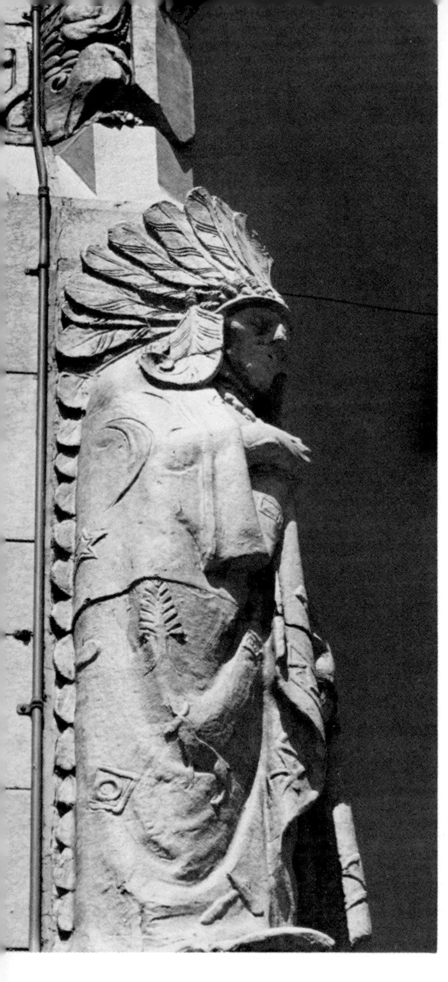

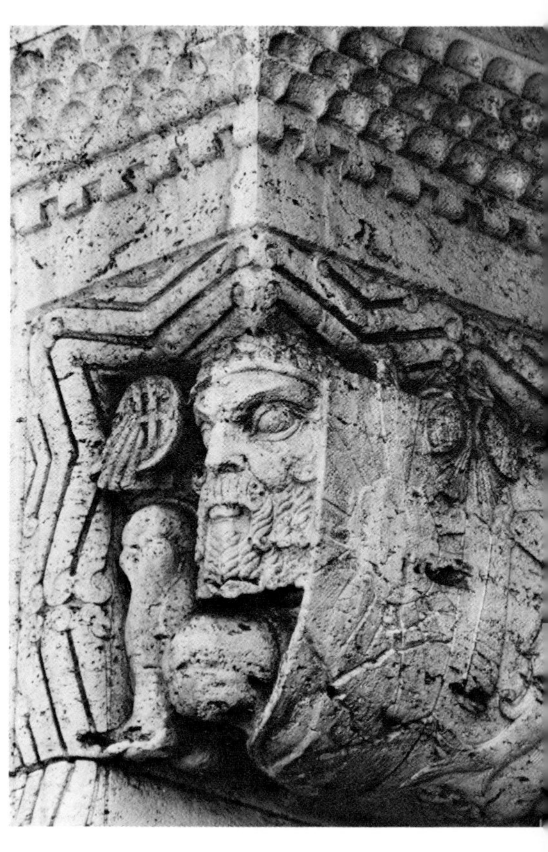

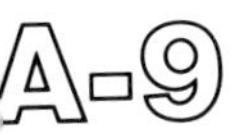

Corrado Joseph Parducci (1900-   )

MICHIGAN NATIONAL BANK RELIEFS

1926, terra cotta, Indian c. 8′, corbel figure 14½″

Michigan National Bank (Grand Rapids Trust Company)
77 Monroe N.W., Monroe Center, Grand Rapids

The Grand Rapids Trust Company Building was designed by Detroit architect Wirt Rowland (1878-1946) of Smith, Hinchman and Grylls. In 1925 the firm had designed a similar building, the Buhl Building in Detroit, which also employed the same architectural modeler, Corrado Joseph Parducci. The general theme of the terra cotta decoration for the Grand Rapids building was the early history of the city and included Indians, tomahawks, canoes, pine trees, wolverines, and other native animals. Located on the corner of the building is the figure of an Indian above which is a lion *sejant* clutching a shield. Flanking the doorway is a medievally inspired corbel figure which clutches a coin. Originally two wolverines perched on top of marble columns also flanked the doorway. The columns, wolverines, and the name of the original bank were removed when the doorway was remodeled by new owners in the early 1940s.

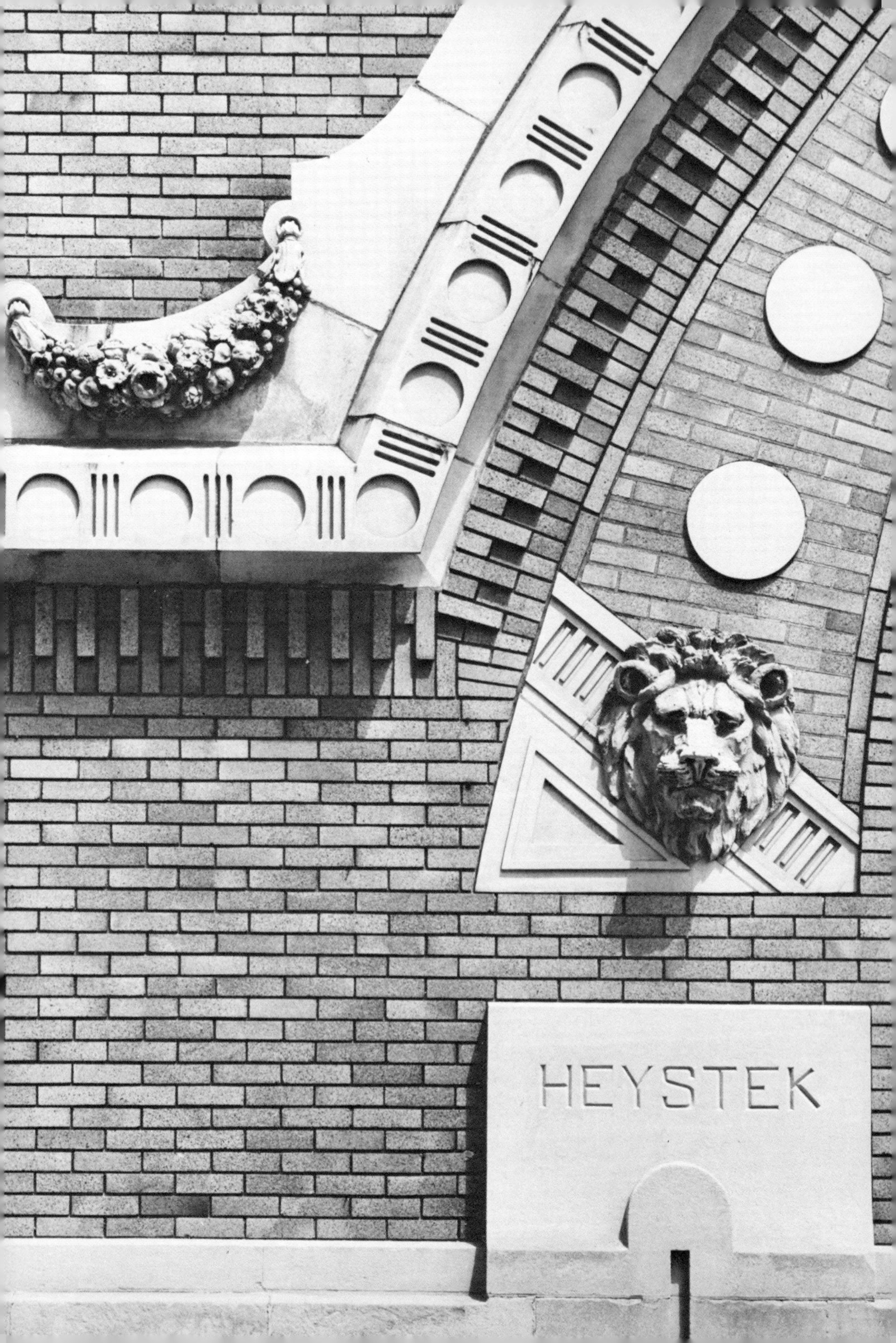
HEYSTEK

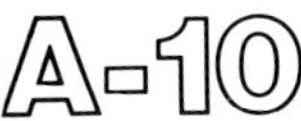

Artist Unknown

LIONS

1910, terra cotta, 3′3″

Heystek Building (Coliseum)
106-14 Commerce Avenue S.W.

The Coliseum opened its doors on November 21, 1910, as a skating rink at a time when skating and sports in general were becoming increasingly popular. In addition to a roller rink, Henry J. Heystek constructed this building to accommodate conventions, exhibitions, meetings, dances, and other events. The elaborate curved arch, which welcomed the coliseum goer, is flanked by garlands and shaggy, expressively modeled lions heads. Above the keystone is an ornate cartouche surrounded by more garlands. The building was purchased in the 1940s for an auto parts stockroom, and is currently used as a parking garage. The large open interior, the classical motifs, and the lions heads are reminiscent of the open air sports arenas of ancient Rome.

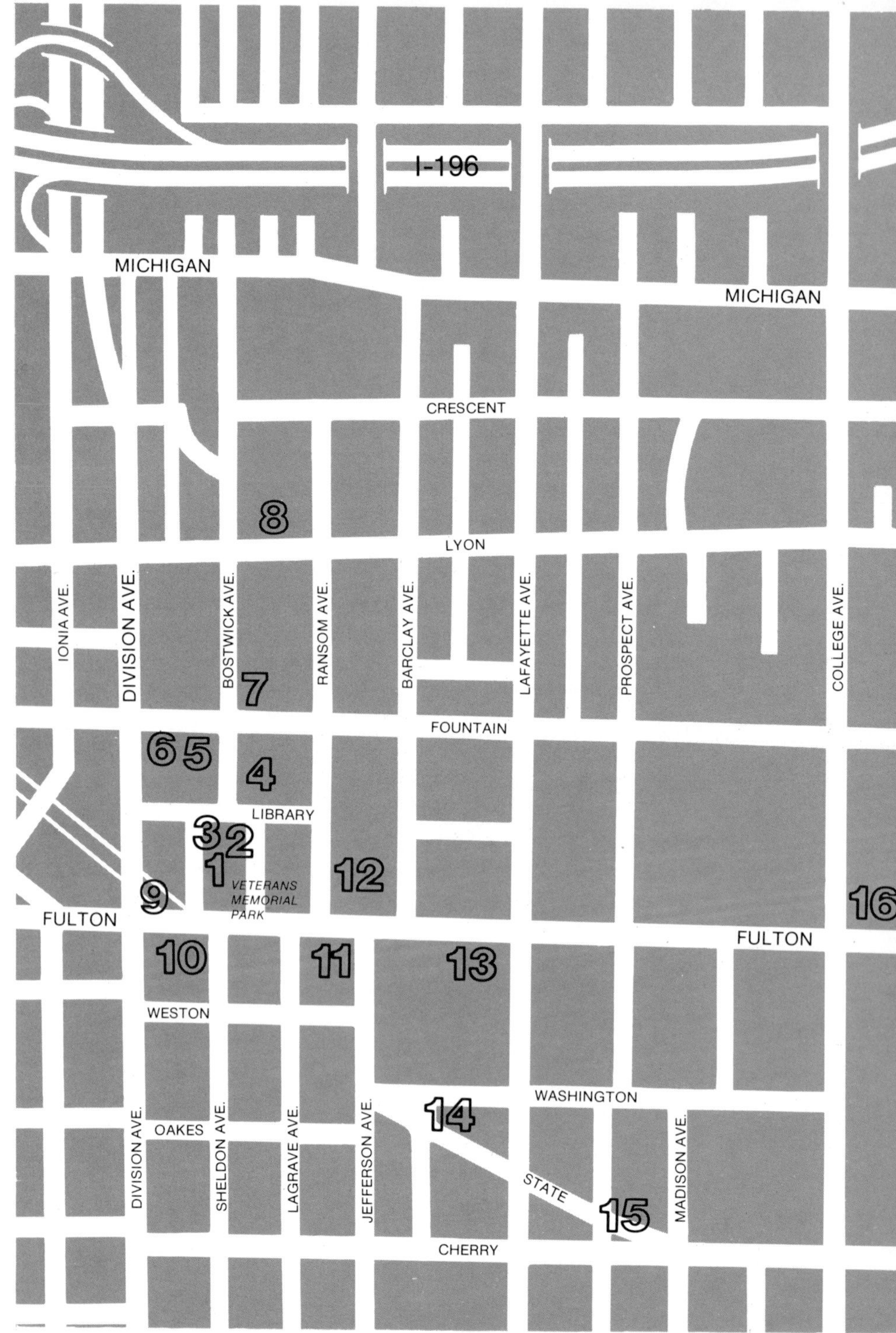

I-196
MICHIGAN
MICHIGAN
CRESCENT
8
LYON
IONIA AVE.
DIVISION AVE.
BOSTWICK AVE.
RANSOM AVE.
BARCLAY AVE.
LAFAYETTE AVE.
PROSPECT AVE.
COLLEGE AVE.
7
FOUNTAIN
6
5
4
LIBRARY
3
2
1
12
VETERANS MEMORIAL PARK
9
16
FULTON
FULTON
10
11
13
WESTON
WASHINGTON
14
DIVISION AVE.
OAKES
SHELDON AVE.
LAGRAVE AVE.
JEFFERSON AVE.
STATE
15
MADISON AVE.
CHERRY

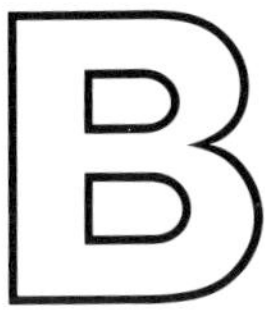

VETERANS MEMORIAL PARK AREA

1. Ralph W. Demmon, MEMORIAL PILLARS
   Veterans Memorial Park
2. Lorado Taft, THOMAS D. GILBERT
   Veterans Memorial Park
3. William Couper, HENRY WADSWORTH LONGFELLOW
   Veterans Memorial Park
4. Thomas Leech, SIZBY
   Grand Rapids Public Library
5. Artist Unknown, SUFFER THE LITTLE CHILDREN
   Fountain Street Church
6. Barbara C. Uhl, UNTITLED
   Fountain Street Church
7. Joseph E. Kinnebrew IV, STROLL
   Grand Rapids Junior College
8. Lumen Martin Winter, THE LEGEND OF GRAND RAPIDS
   Gerald R. Ford Health Center, Grand Rapids Junior College
9. Leon Coquard (?), SOLDIERS' MONUMENT
   Monument Park
10. Artist Unknown, DOLPHIN RELIEF
    Ladies Literary Club
11. Artist Unknown, PEACOCKS
    Willard Building
12. Artist Unknown, SAINT CECILIA RELIEFS
    Saint Cecilia Music Society Building
13. Jasha Green, FLOOR KITE XIV
    Grand Rapids Art Museum
14. Adolph A. Weinman, ABRAHAM LINCOLN
    Lincoln Place
15. Theodore Alice Ruggles Kitson, THE HIKER
    Foster Park
16. B. Wathof and Son, ROOSTER WEATHERVANE
    Central Reformed Church

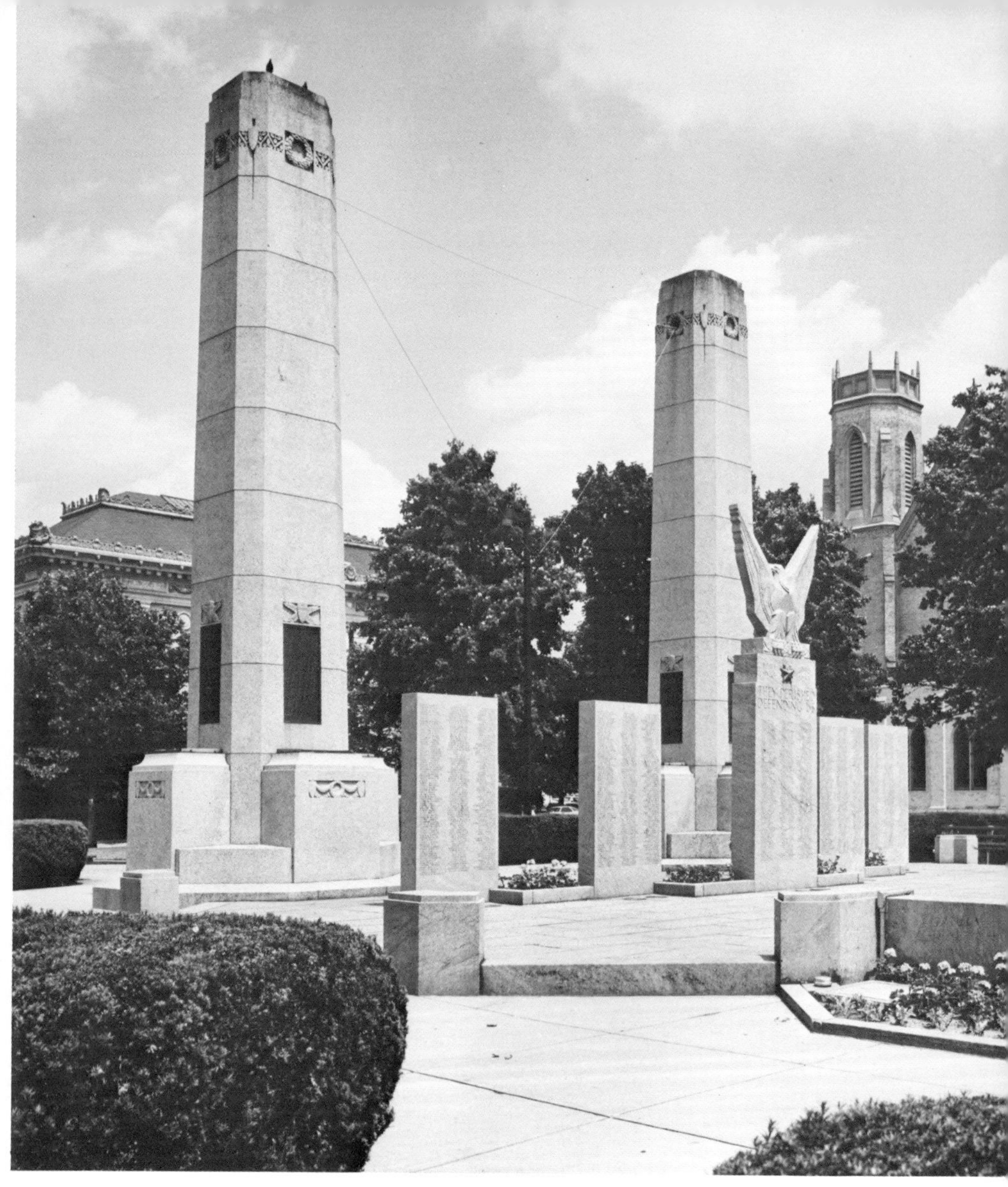

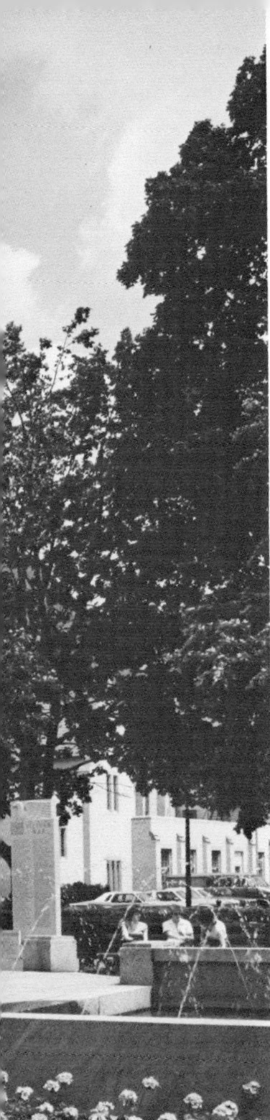

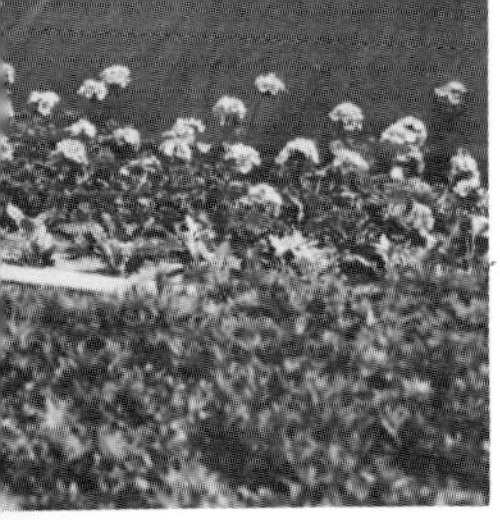

B-1

Ralph W. Demmon (1894-1978), Designer

MEMORIAL PILLARS

1926, granite, 35′

Veterans Memorial Park (Fulton Street Park)
Fulton, Sheldon, Library, and Park Place, Grand Rapids

After World War I there was a move to erect a war memorial in the form of a building which could include an art gallery, war museum, and auditorium. It was decided, however, to erect memorial pillars or pylons inscribed with the names of the dead to replace the temporary memorial pillars which had been placed in Fulton Street Park during the war. The memorial was designed by Grand Rapids architect Ralph W. Demmon (1894-1978) and the choice of design is explained in the dedication booklet as follows: "the memorial is designed after the spirit of Egyptian architecture which obtained in that country after the expulsion of the barbarous Hyskos tribes, or Shepherd kings, and symbolize a new freedom and a new hope." Fulton Street Park, renamed Veterans Memorial Park in 1956, was selected as the site not only because of the previous pillars, but because this park had served as a courthouse and public square since 1833. Funds were provided by the people of Grand Rapids and the monument was dedicated on Armistice Day, November 11, 1926. In 1957 five stelae, carved by F. C. Ruppel and S. J. Terhaar, were added to commemorate those who had given their lives in World War II and the Korean War. Again, in 1975, two more stelae were added in memory of those who had died in the Vietnam War.

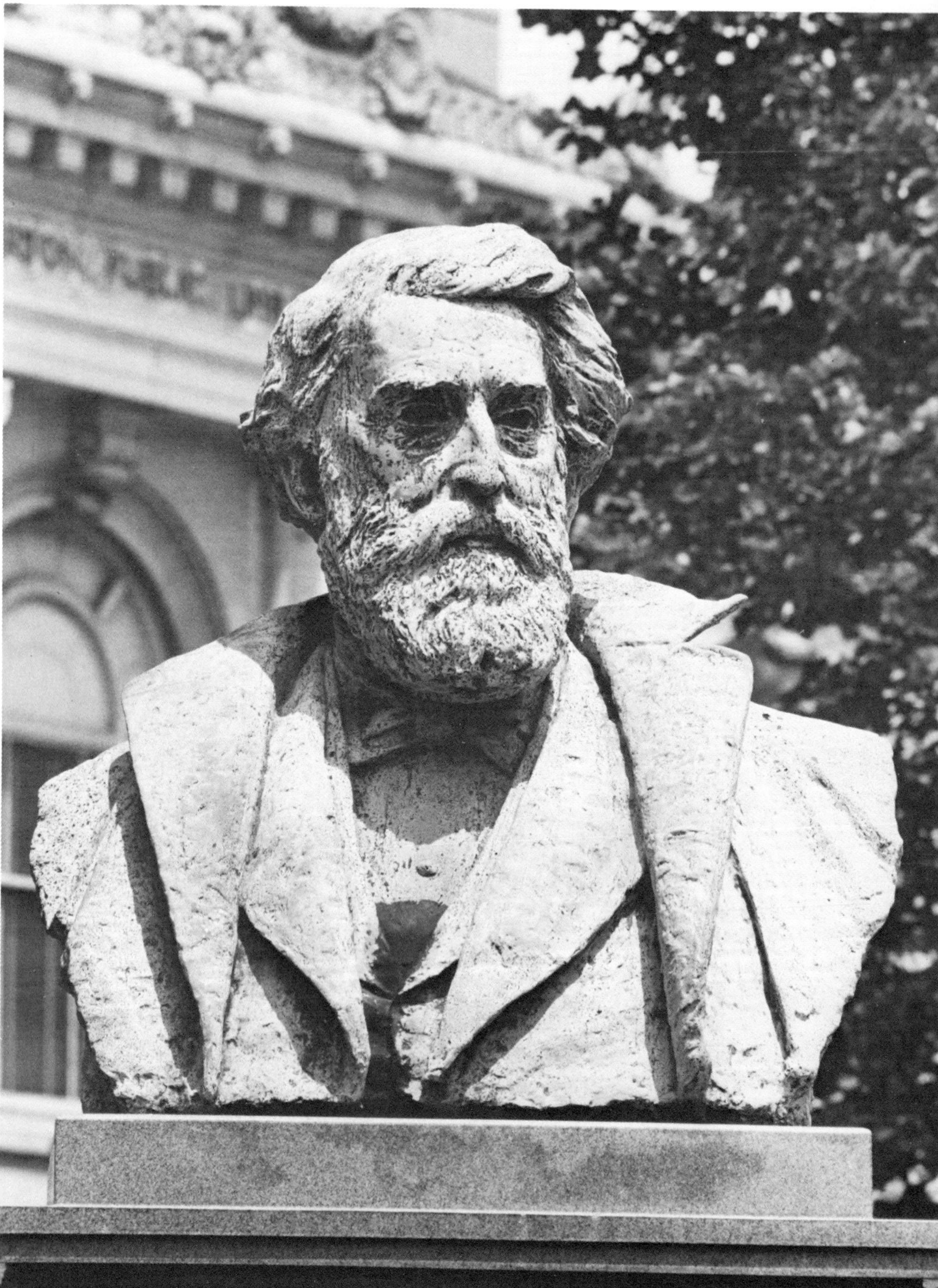

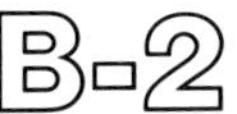

Lorado Taft (1860-1936)

THOMAS D. GILBERT

1895, bronze, 4′

[L. Taft Sc 95]

Veterans Memorial Park (Fulton Street Park)
Fulton, Sheldon, Library, and Park Place, Grand Rapids

During impressive dedication ceremonies on June 5, 1896, the bust of Thomas D. Gilbert (1815-1894) was unveiled. The statue was erected by former business associates of the City National Bank and the Grand Rapids Gas Company. Gilbert, a businessman, came to Grand Rapids in 1855 and held many civic positions including sheriff, alderman, and state legislator. Known for his generosity, Gilbert personally took over the care of Fulton Street Park after it was abandoned as a county courthouse square. He fenced in the grounds to keep out cattle and swine, built walks, cultivated the soil, and planted trees. The textured bust of Gilbert, whose hair and coat lapels are slightly ruffled by the wind, was modeled by the noted American sculptor Lorado Taft. It is fitting that the watchful eye of Gilbert continues to gaze intently over the park.

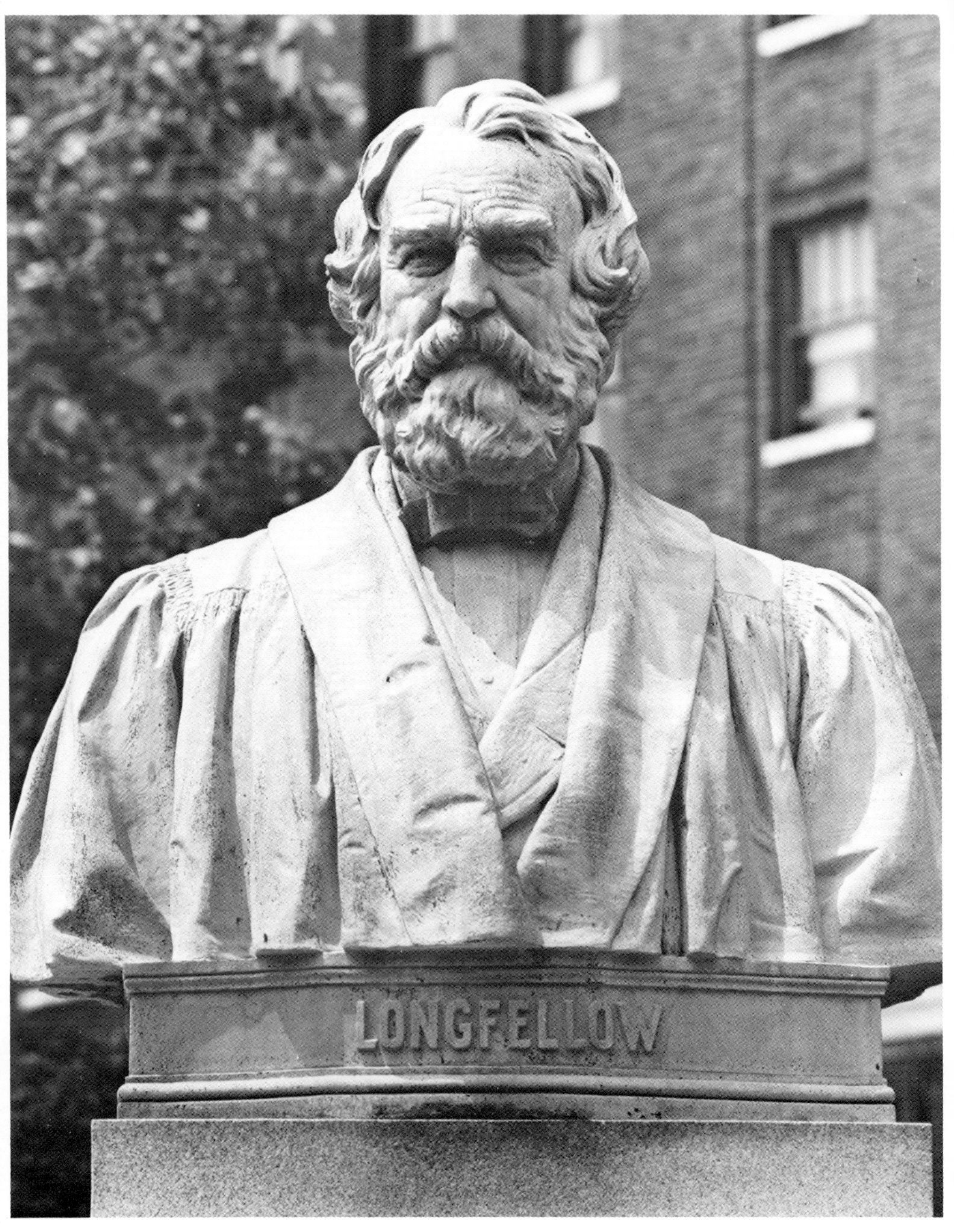
LONGFELLOW

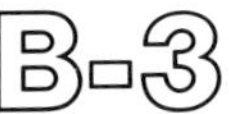

William Couper (1854-1942)

HENRY WADSWORTH LONGFELLOW

1912, bronze, 3'10"

[Wm Couper New York]

Veterans Memorial Park (Fulton Street Park)
Fulton, Sheldon, Library, and Park Place, Grand Rapids

William Couper's bust of Henry Wadsworth Longfellow was given to the city by Frederick and Loraine Pratt Immen. It complements Lorado Taft's bust of Thomas D. Gilbert which was placed in the opposite corner of the park in 1896 (see p. 43). Loraine Pratt Immen (1840-1927) was a singular woman who made many contributions to the cultural life of Grand Rapids. Some of her other gifts include Adolph A. Weinman's bust of Lincoln for Lincoln Park (see p. 67) and Tiffany windows for Park Congregational Church and the Ladies Literary Club. At the dedication ceremonies on June 22, 1912, Immen, who was active in the Ladies Literary Club, spoke on *Longfellow, the Poet and Citizen.* She remarked that she had chosen Longfellow because he was the beloved poet of America. Longfellow (1807-1882) was a noted nineteenth century American author whose writings include *Evangeline* and *Hiawatha.* He taught at Harvard College from 1835 to 1854 and is protrayed in academic gown. He is similarly portrayed in a seated statue located in Washington, D.C., which was begun by Thomas Ball (1819-1911) and completed by Couper in 1909.

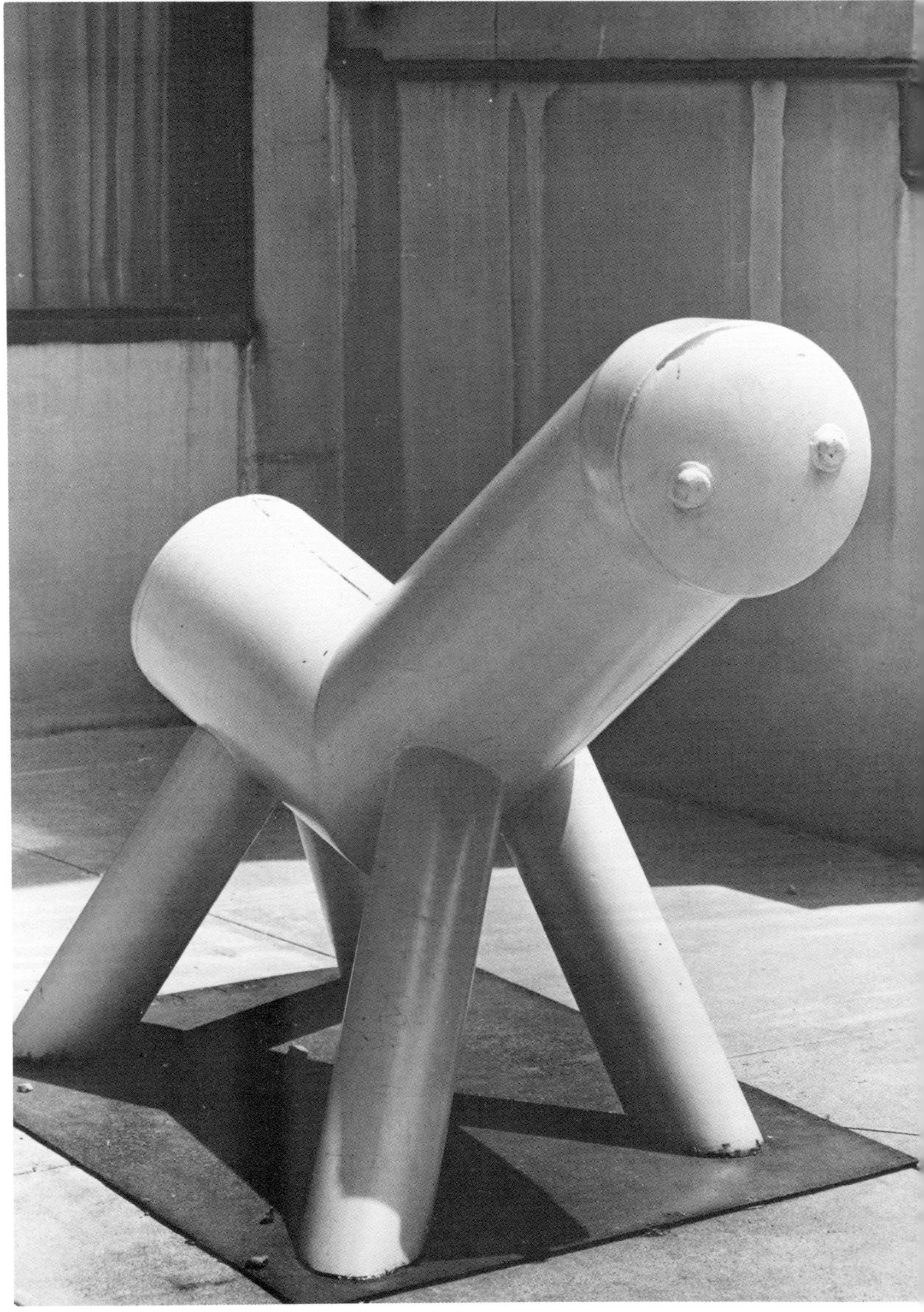

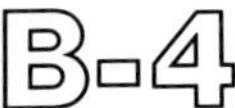

Thomas Leech (c. 1951-   )

SIZBY

1973, steel, 4′

[TL 1973]

Grand Rapids Public Library
60 Library Plaza N.E., Grand Rapids

This play sculpture is a gift of Urban Concerns, Inc., who commissioned the work, and the artist, Thomas Leech. It was designed for the children at the Grand Rapids Public Library and is located outside the Children's Room. A contest was held to name the gangly baby animal, and William Alexander submitted the winning name of Sizby. *Sizby* is composed of water tanks and other cylindrical forms which are painted yellow.

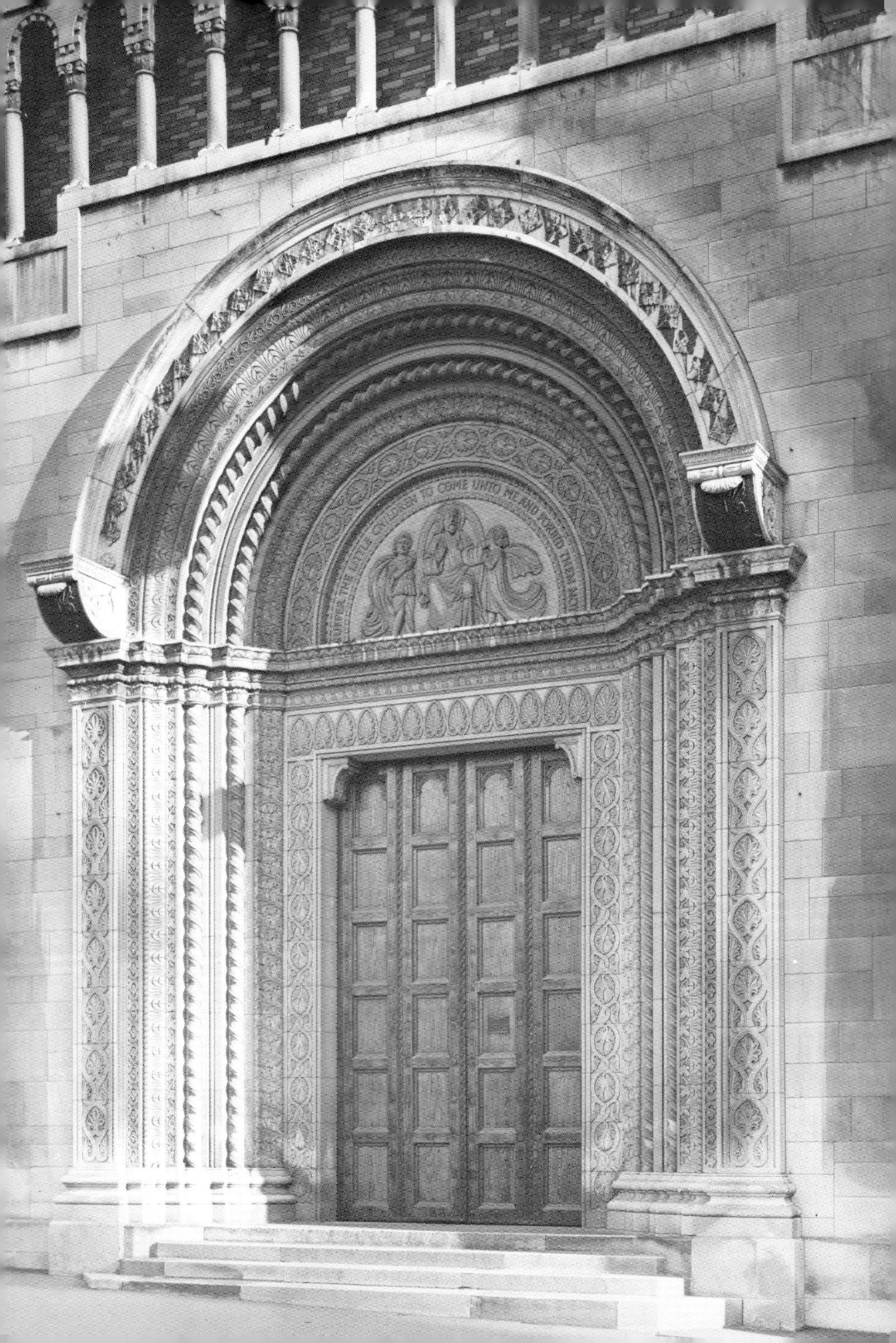
SUFFER THE LITTLE CHILDREN TO COME UNTO ME AND FORBID THEM NO

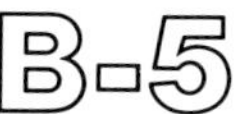

Artist Unknown

SUFFER THE LITTLE CHILDREN

c. 1922, limestone, 7′11″

Fountain Street Church
24 Fountain N.E., Grand Rapids

In 1825 the Reverend Isaac McCoy founded the Thomas Mission on the banks of the Grand River near what is today the corner of West Bridge and Front Streets. This Indian mission was the predecessor of the Fountain Street Baptist Church which today is interdenominational. When the previous building burned down in 1917, Dr. Alfred W. Wishart, pastor from 1906 to 1933, supervised the construction of this Lombard Romanesque church which was designed by Coolidge and Hodgdon of Chicago and dedicated on February 3, 1924. Sculpture and other symbolic Christian art has been incorporated into this building which has also served as a cultural center and public forum for controversial issues. The tympanum of this recessed entryway portrays the invitation found in Luke 18:16 to "suffer the little children to come unto me and forbid them not." This scene is surrounded by foliage including honeysuckle and acanthus, symbolic of the resurrection and heaven. This relief and others, including peacocks drinking from the Fountain of Life, were carved by the Furst Kerber Cut Stone Company of Bedford, Indiana.

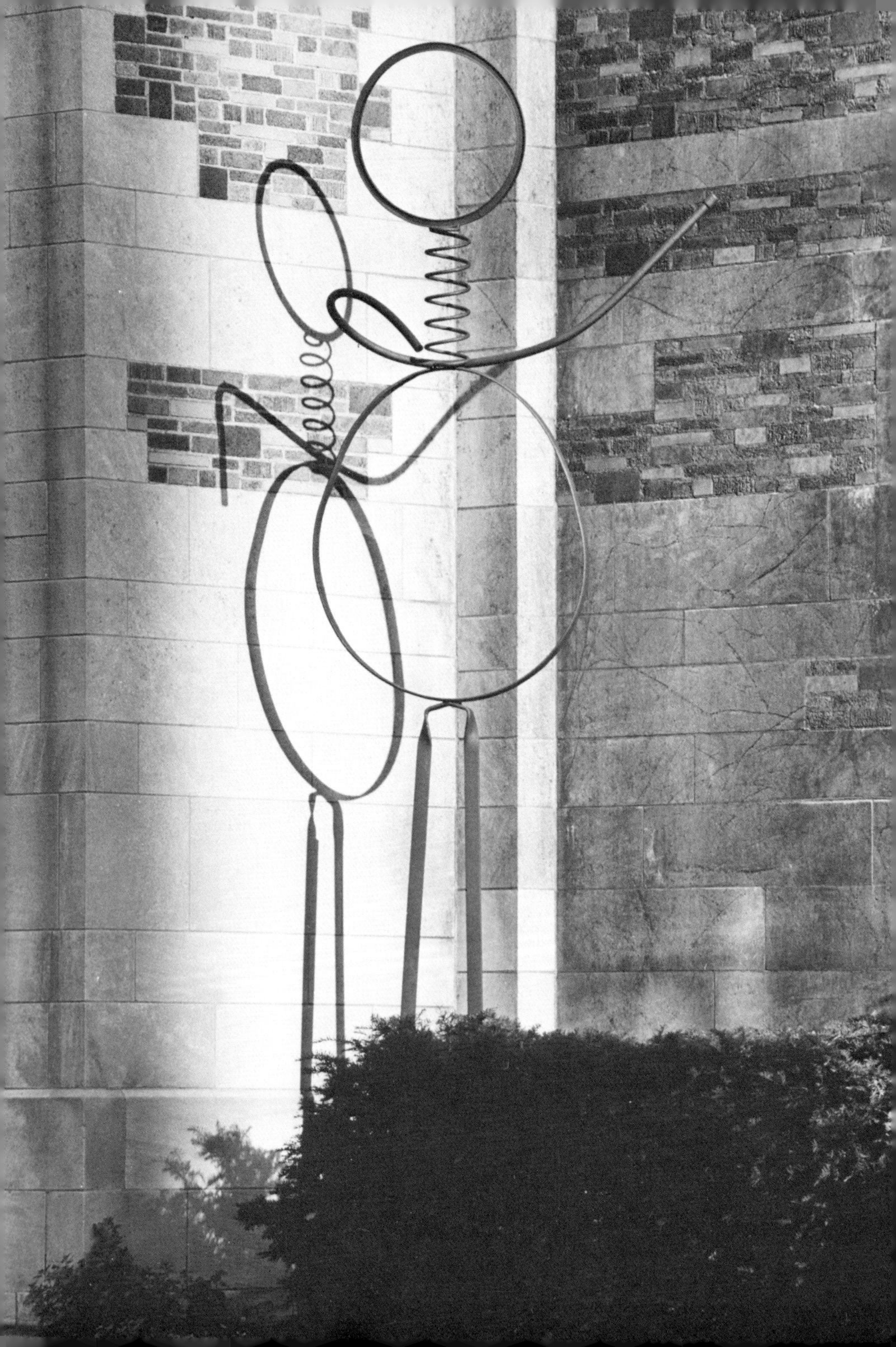

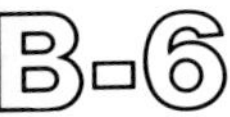

Barbara (Bobbie) C. Uhl (1925-)

UNTITLED

1975, iron, 17′6″

Fountain Street Church
24 Fountain N.E., Grand Rapids

This sculpture is a spatial linear drawing which has been painted brick red. A gift of the artist and Urban Concerns, Inc., it was dedicated on June 11, 1978. The sculpture was originally conceived as a totem which represented one of Barbara Uhl's sons and was part of a group of family totems. It now is purposefully untitled to encourage a variety of imaginative responses from the viewer. The figure, which jiggles and dances when touched, speaks to the need for play in everyone. It is sometimes joined by a playmate created through day and nighttime shadows.

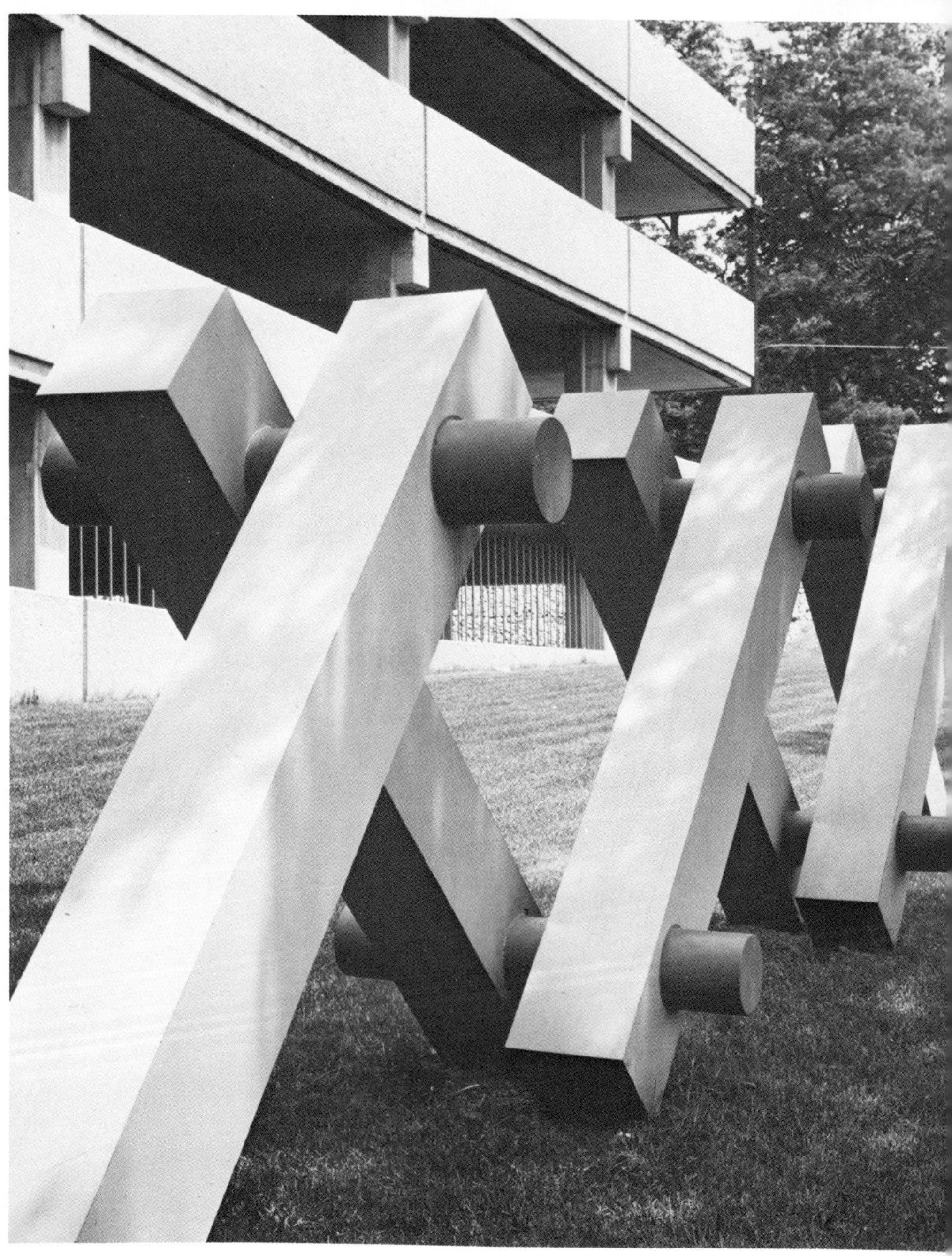

B-7

Joseph E. Kinnebrew IV (1942-)

STROLL

c. 1973, steel, 8′

[JK 74]

Grand Rapids Junior College Parking Ramp
Fountain and Bostwick N.E.

Stroll was displayed at the Grand Rapids Art Museum in 1973 as part of the exhibition, *Four American Sculptors.* The exhibition featured Grand Rapids sculptors and ran concurrently with another exhibition, *Sculpture Off the Pedestal,* which gained national attention for Grand Rapids. This giant green toy was purchased after the exhibition by Grand Rapids Junior College and placed near their parking ramp. Composed of diagonal beams which are joined by pegs, this work contrasts with the static horizontality of the ramp as it ambles along the grass.

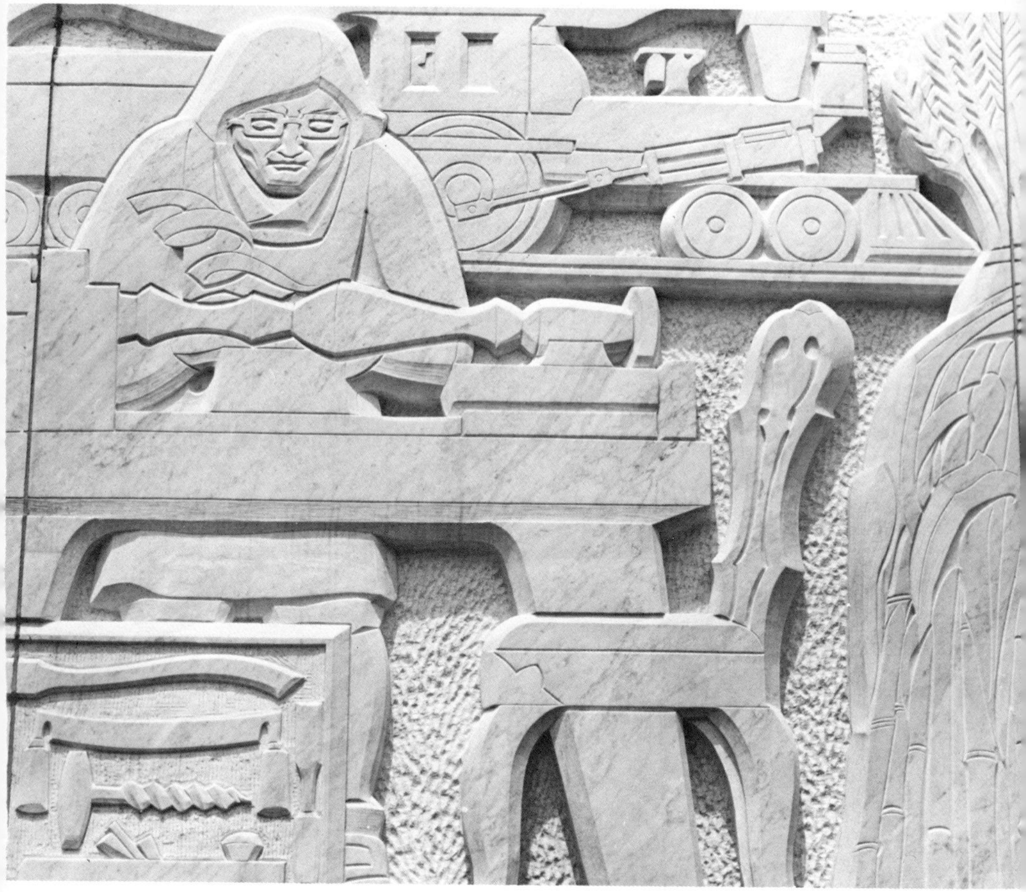

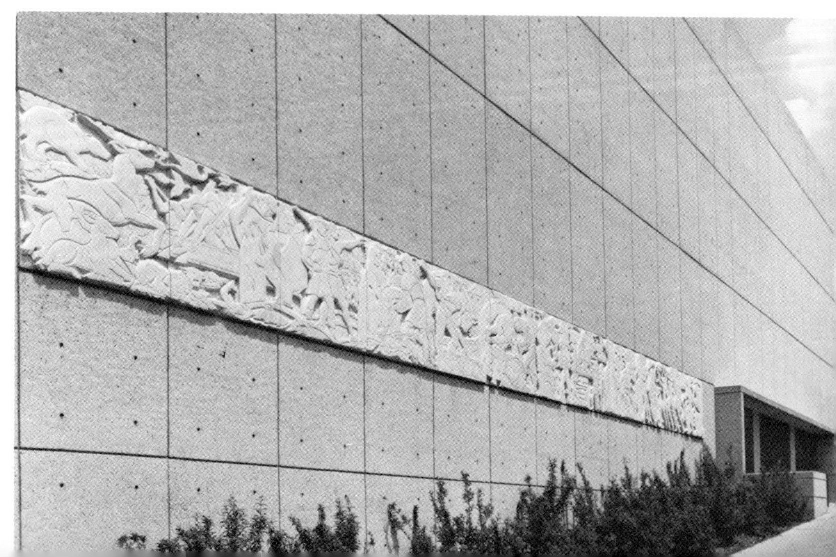

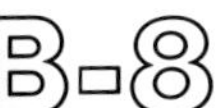

Lumen Martin Winter (1908-)

THE LEGEND OF GRAND RAPIDS

1976, marble, 5′

[Lumen Winter Studios of A. Pierotti 1976]

Gerald R. Ford Health Center, Grand Rapids Junior College
Lyon and Ransom N.E., Grand Rapids

This sixty foot frieze tells the story of Grand Rapids from its earliest beginnings to the present, beginning on the left with a primeval forest through which Indians are paddling a canoe. The coming of the white man to Michigan is marked by a Jesuit missionary, Antoine de la Mothe Cadillac arriving in a boat, and Henry H. Schoolcraft exploring the territory with an Indian guide. Early Grand Rapids settlers include Louis Campau, who set up a trading post on the banks of the Grand River, and the surveyor John Ball. The arts of civilization follow and include lumbering, milling, black smithing, furniture making, transportation, and farming. The right side of the frieze portrays dance, music, athletics, and education. Funds for the sculptural relief were provided by the Grand Rapids Board of Education, which commissioned the work, and by private donations. Students from Grand Rapids Junior College joined Lumen Winter in Italy to help with the carving. The commission was an immensely satisfying one for Winter who spent his early life in Grand Rapids and is a graduate of Grand Rapids Junior College. Both former President Gerald R. Ford, who also lived in Grand Rapids, and Winter were part of the ceremonies when the Gerald R. Ford Health and Education Center was dedicated on November 1, 1976.

Leon Coquard (1860-1923), Designer (?)

SOLDIERS' MONUMENT

c. 1885, white bronze, 34′

Monument Park
Fulton and Division, Monroe Center, Grand Rapids

On February 13, 1864, the Kent County Soldiers' Monument Association was organized but was unable to raise enough funds to erect a memorial to the soldiers and sailors who had fought in the Civil War. Interest in a monument was revived when the Army of the Cumberland announced that their Annual Reunion would be held in Grand Rapids in 1885. The Detroit Bronze Company provided additional impetus by suggesting that a monument be cast in their highly touted, but relatively inexpensive, white bronze. Park land, which had been acquired in 1843, was set aside in 1884 for the monument and dedication ceremonies were held on September 17, 1885 as part of the reunion. Detroit architect Leon Coquard, (1860-1923), whose name is on a drawing of the monument which appeared on the front page of the Grand Rapids *Daily Democrat* on September 11, 1885, may have designed the monument.

The layers of this Victorian cake, which is topped by an individual soldier, include portraits of Lincoln, Grant, Farragut, and Garfield; cherubs which spout water; the names and dates of engagements in which Kent County soldiers fought; a scene, "Women's Mission of Mercy," which portrays a woman giving aid to a wounded soldier; and quotations from Lincoln, Jackson, Grant, and Garfield. In addition to fund raising, other problems have beset this monument, sometimes referred to as the "tin soldier" or the "zinc toothpick," including a move to replace it and the whittling away of the park to its present petite size. Originally grey, this Confederate color was considered inappropriate for the boys who had fought in blue, and in recent years, the monument has been painted Union blue.

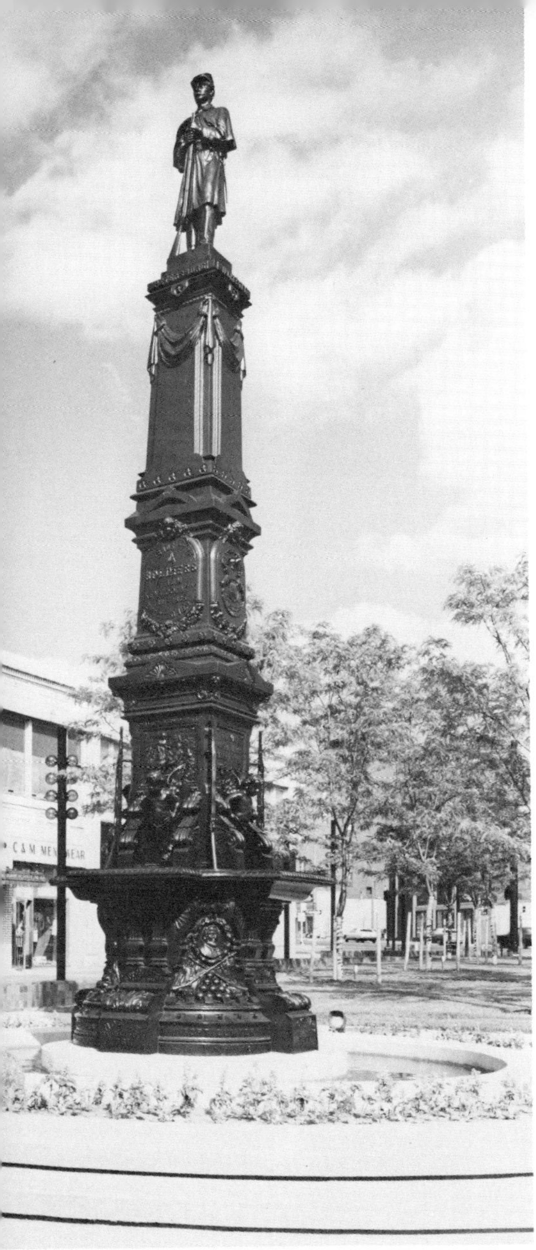

B-9

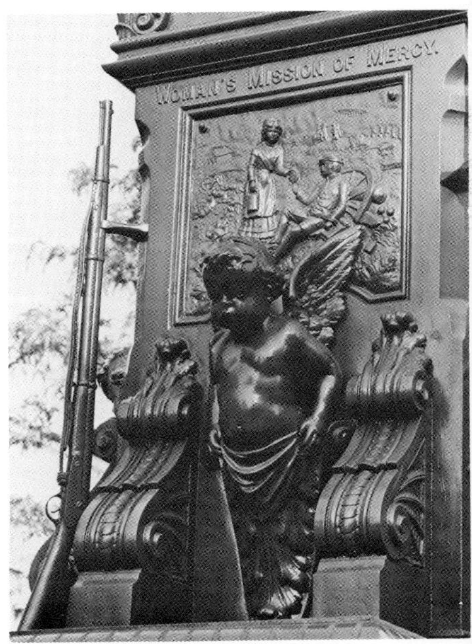

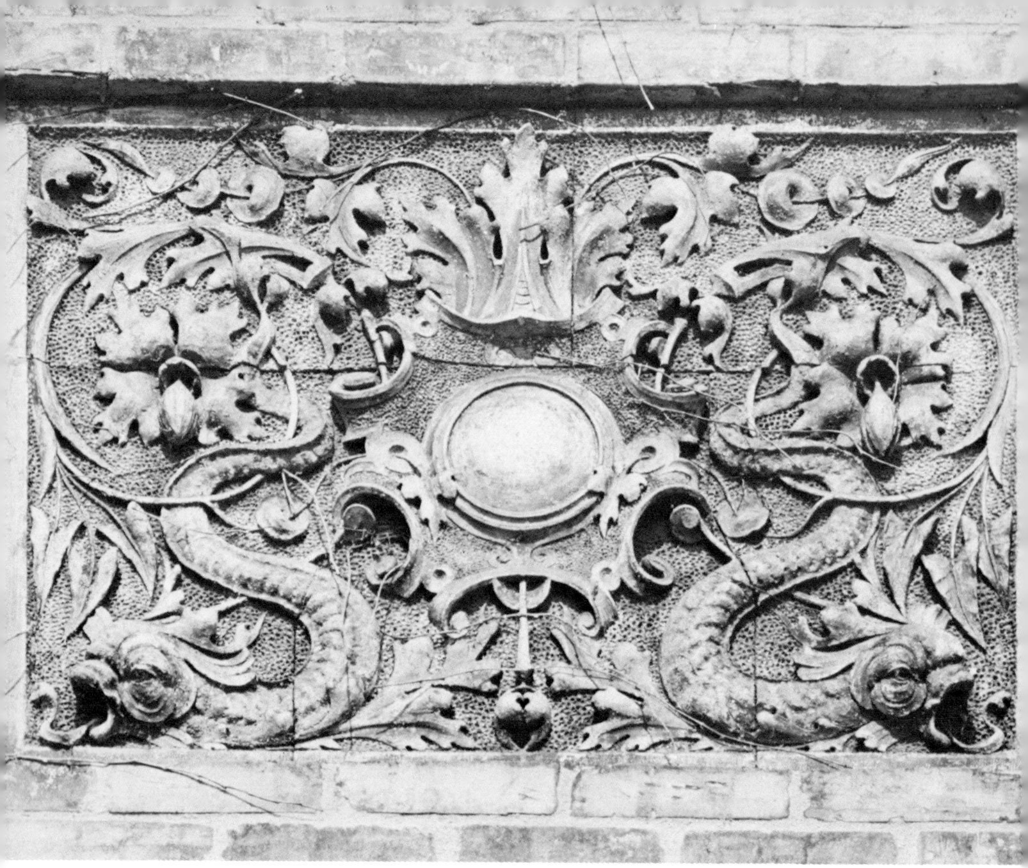

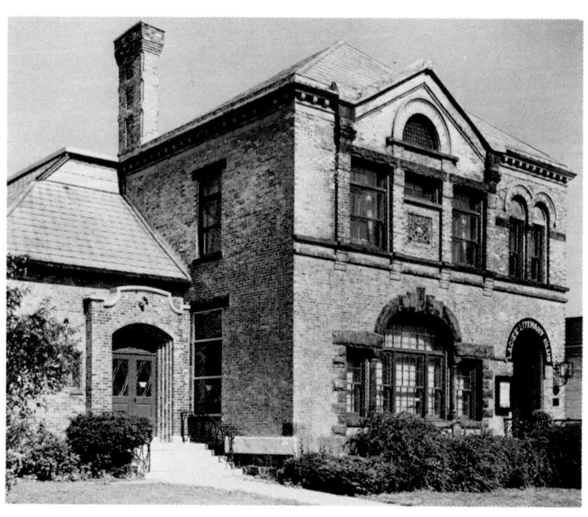

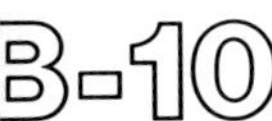

Artist Unknown

DOLPHIN RELIEF

1887, terra cotta, c. 30″

Ladies Literary Club
61 Sheldon S.E., Grand Rapids

The Ladies Literary Club, an outgrowth of the Ladies Reading Club of 1869, was organized in 1882 to study history, art, science, and literature. In 1887 the women's club built their present building which was designed by Grand Rapids architect William G. Robinson (1835-1907). The building is one of the earliest in the United States to be constructed specifically for a women's clubhouse and it reflects the burgeoning women's club movement in the nineteenth century. When the building committee approved the design, they specified that an additional $25.00 be spent for a terra cotta ornament for the front of the building. That allocation quite likely refers to this terra cotta relief which portrays two dolphins swimming through a sea of foliage. Dolphins have been a familiar art motif since antiquity and have been particularly popular in recent centuries as parts of furniture or architectural decoration. Besides the Ladies Literary Club, dolphins can also be found on two other Victorian buildings located on nearby Ionia Avenue. They are the William Alden Smith Building and the Waldron Building, both constructed in 1894.

Artist Unknown

PEACOCKS

1930, terra cotta, c. 2′

Willard Building
E. Fulton and Jefferson S. E., Grand Rapids

The Willard Building was named after Dr. Willard M. Burleson by his wife and daughter. The building, which was constructed to house several commercial shops, stands on the site of the Burleson Hospital. The roofline of this L-shaped building is rhythmically punctuated with exquisitely colored peacocks which speak of another era. For with the coming of the depression and modern architecture, buildings with terra cotta decoration were no longer constructed.

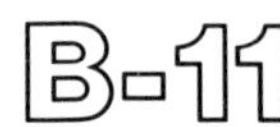

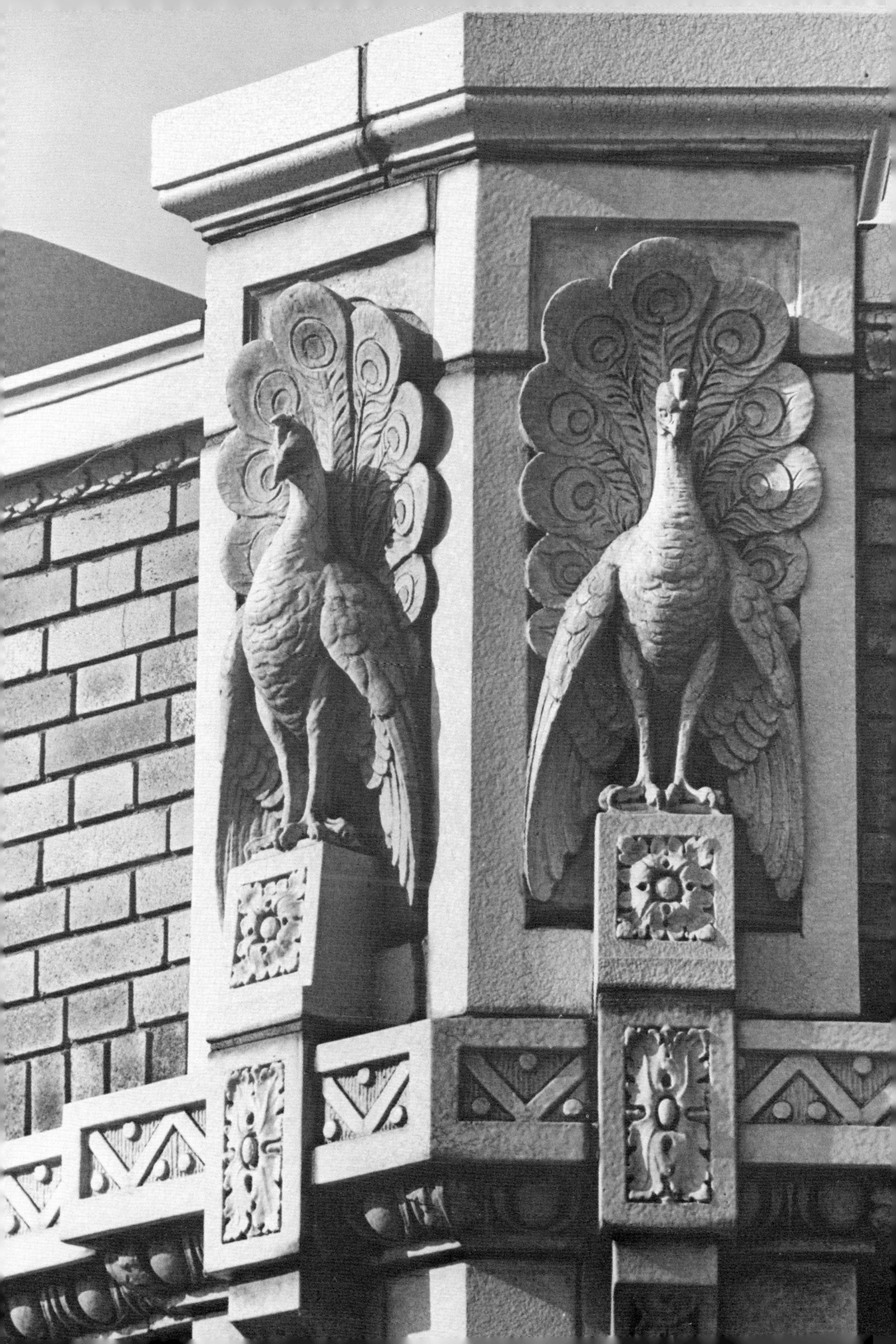

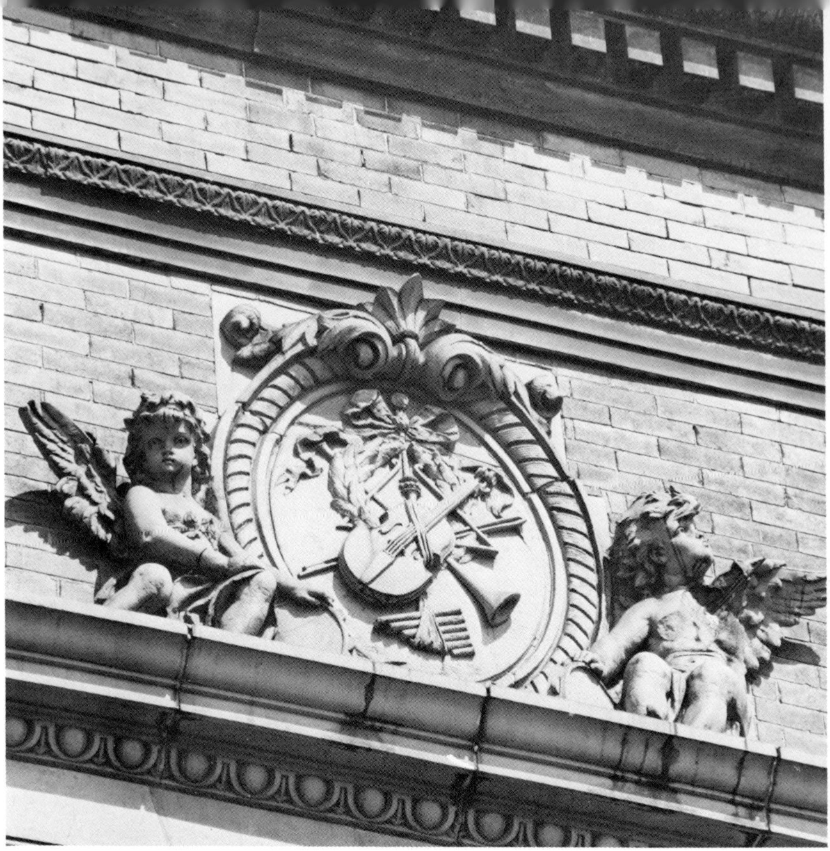

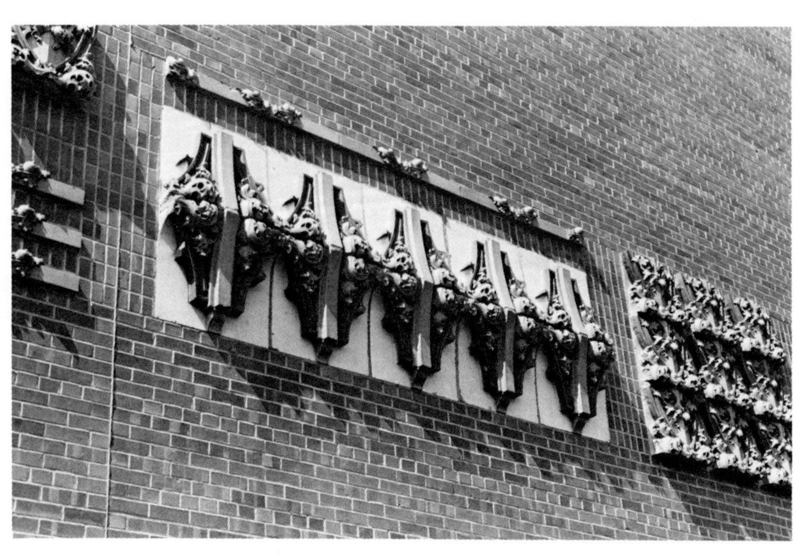

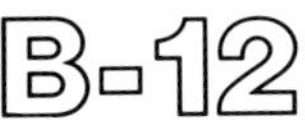

Artist Unknown

SAINT CECILIA RELIEFS

c. 1894, terra cotta, cartouche c. 4′

Artist Unknown

METZ BUILDING RELIEFS

c. 1912, terra cotta, c. 4′

Saint Cecilia Music Society Building
24 Ransom N.E., Grand Rapids

The Saint Cecilia Music Society was founded by nine women in 1883 for the sole purpose of music. On June 19, 1894, the Society dedicated its new Renaissance Revival building which was designed by Henry Ives Cobb (1859-1931) of Chicago. This is the first building in the United States to be built by women for the exclusive use of music. The Society is named after Saint Cecilia who was martyred for her Christian faith and later became patron saint of music and musicians. Saint Cecilia was a woman of such remarkable musical ability that an angel often attended her. She composed hymns, sang sweetly, could play any instrument, and is credited with the invention of the organ. The terra cotta cartouche, which contains musical instruments and is flanked by cherubs, reflects the musical interests of the Society.

The right side of the building contains polychrome terra cotta decoration from the Metz Building which was designed by Grand Rapids architect William R. Clarke around 1912. When the Metz Building was razed in 1971, the Kent County Council for Historic Preservation preserved the facade and a portion of the foliate ornamentation was used to relieve the large brick expanse on the south side of the building.

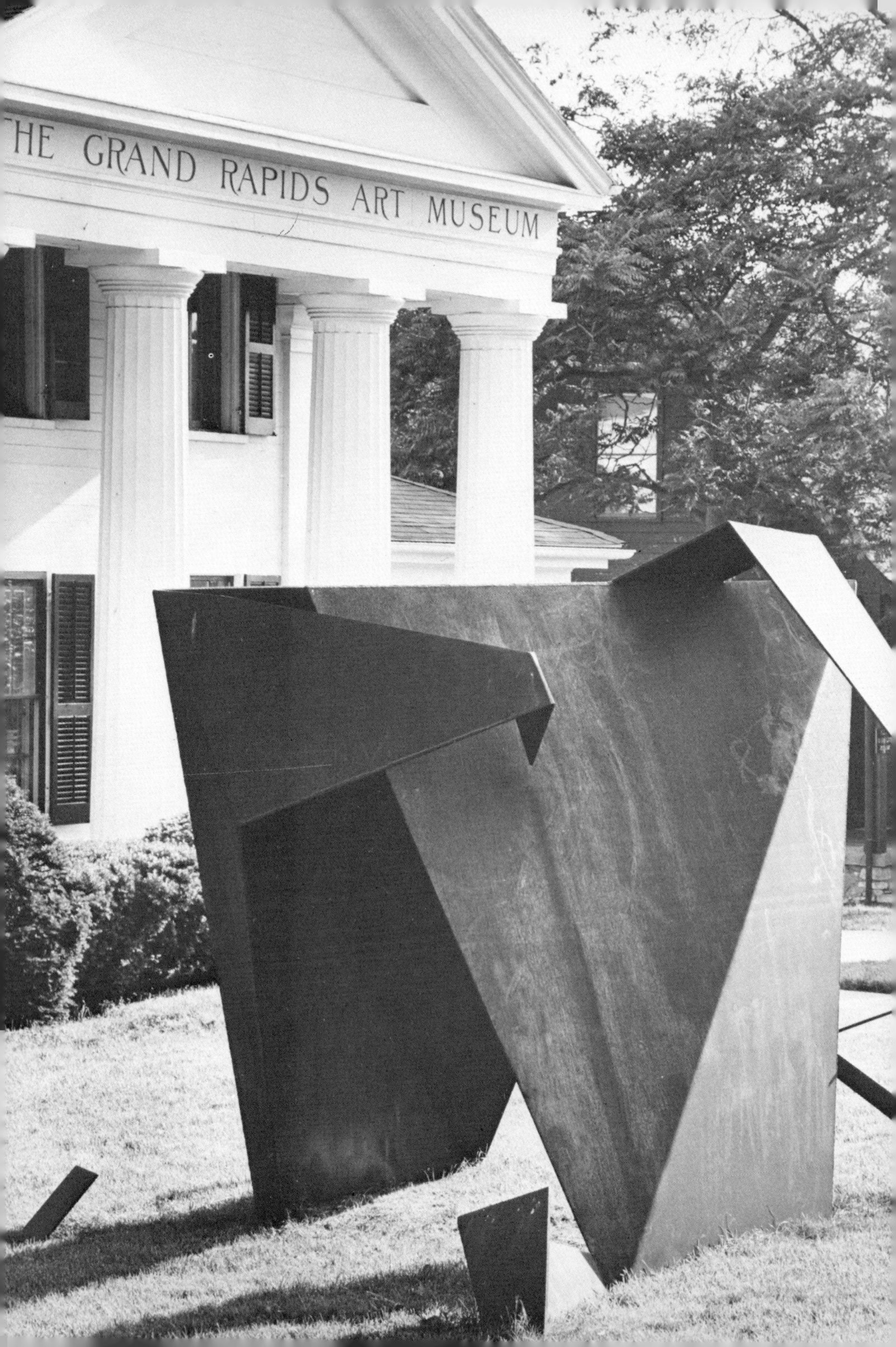
THE GRAND RAPIDS ART MUSEUM

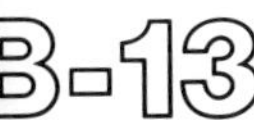

Jasha Green (1927-   )

FLOOR KITE XIV

1977, cor-ten steel, 8′9″

Grand Rapids Art Museum
230 E. Fulton, Grand Rapids

In 1977, Jasha Green created four floor kites for an exhibition jointly sponsored by the Chrysler Museum, Norfolk, Virginia, and the Virginia Beach Arts Center. *Floor Kite XIV* was subsequently purchased by Percy Berman, Grand Rapids, for the Grand Rapids Art Museum. Green began his kite series in 1976 with the construction of *Floor Kite I.* In this series, Green has challenged the nature of steel by creating kites which appear to be made of folded paper. *Floor Kite XIV* is composed of large planes which enclose space. Folded appendages reach out from the planes and add to the sense of hovering motion.

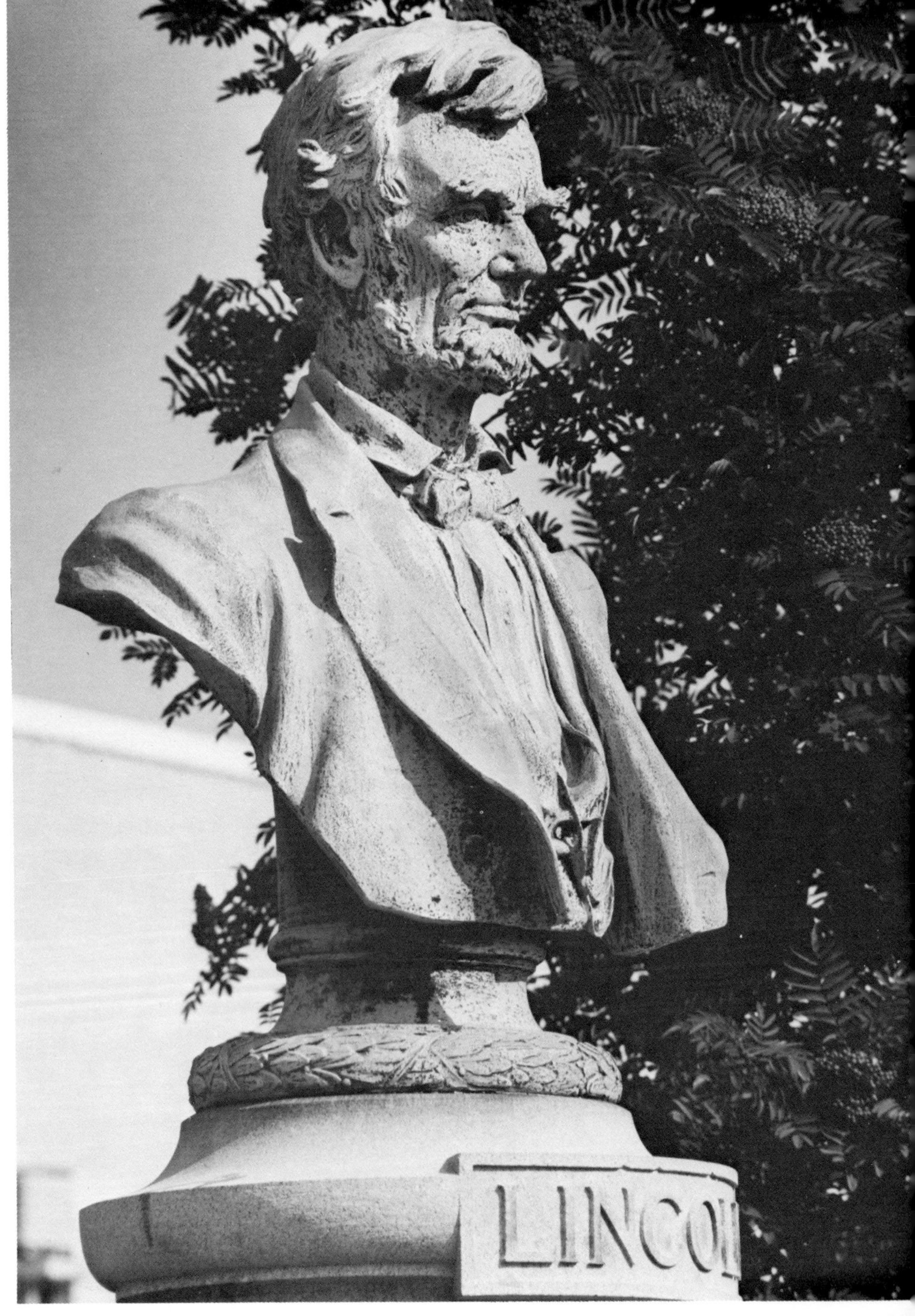
LINCO

B-14

Adolph A. Weinman (1870-1952)

ABRAHAM LINCOLN

c. 1913, bronze, 4'2"

[A A Weinman Sc   Gorham Co. Founders]

Lincoln Place (State Street Park)
State and Washington S.E., Grand Rapids

Loraine Pratt Immen presented the bust of Abraham Lincoln to the city on June 2, 1913, for the small triangular park which had been renamed Lincoln Place in honor of the new sculpture. Mrs. Immen had previously offered to make the initial contribution for a full-length statue of Lincoln to replace the *Soldiers' Monument* in Monument Park. Lincoln was an enormously popular subject for statuary and Adolph Weinman had already created two full-length statues of Lincoln shortly before he modeled this gaunt, brooding figure of Lincoln. The other two statues of Lincoln are located in Hodgenville and Frankfort, Kentucky. In the 1970s the Greek Revival Law Office of Charles P. Calkins was moved to the park and the bust of this famous lawyer was turned around to face the building.

Theodore Alice Ruggles Kitson (1871-1932)

THE HIKER

c. 1927, bronze, 8′5″

Foster Park
State and Cherry S.E., Grand Rapids

The hiker, so called because of his long hikes in the hot steaming jungles, fought in the name of freedom, humanity, and patriotism in Cuba, the Philippine Islands, and in a relief expedition to China during the Boxer Rebellion. The romanticized treatment of this foot soldier suggests the popularity of "this splendid little war," the Spanish-American War of 1898-1902, in which the United States emerged as a world power and expanded its territories to include Puerto Rico, Guam, and the Philippine Islands. The freed colonies are represented in the cruciform plaque on the boulder by a woman who kneels before a soldier and a sailor while the U.S.S. *Maine* floats in the background. Funds for the monument were raised through the efforts of the Guy V. Henry Camp No. 3, United Spanish War Veterans, and dedication ceremonies were held on April 28, 1928, at Lookout Park. In 1957, *The Hiker* was moved to its downtown location in Foster Park. Approximately fifty other castings of *The Hiker* can be found throughout the United States, including the original which was erected at the University of Minnesota in 1906. Two others can be found in the Michigan cities of Kalamazoo (c. 1923) and Lansing (c. 1945).

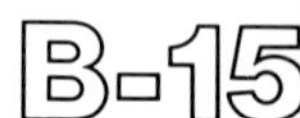

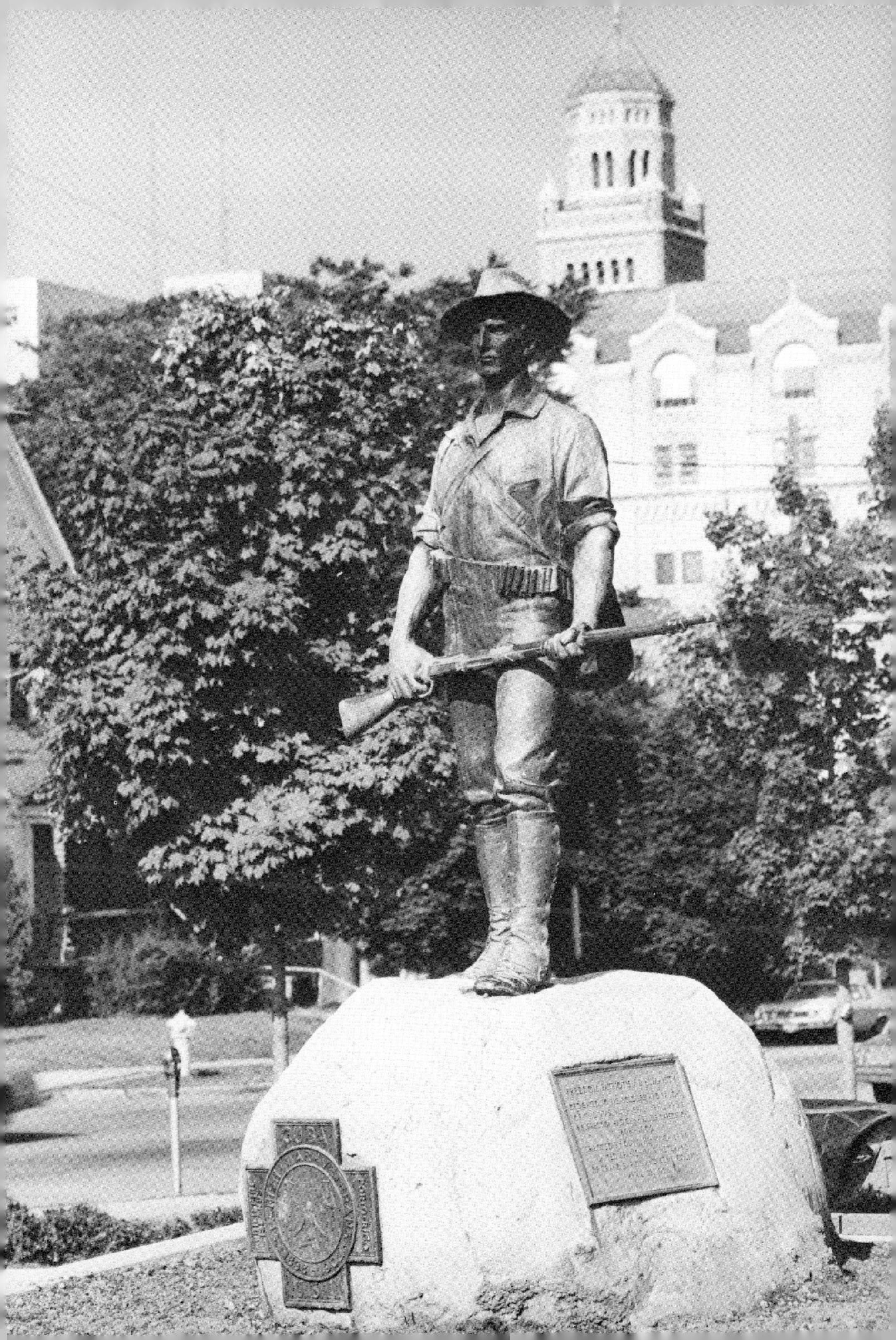
CUBA
PORTO RICO

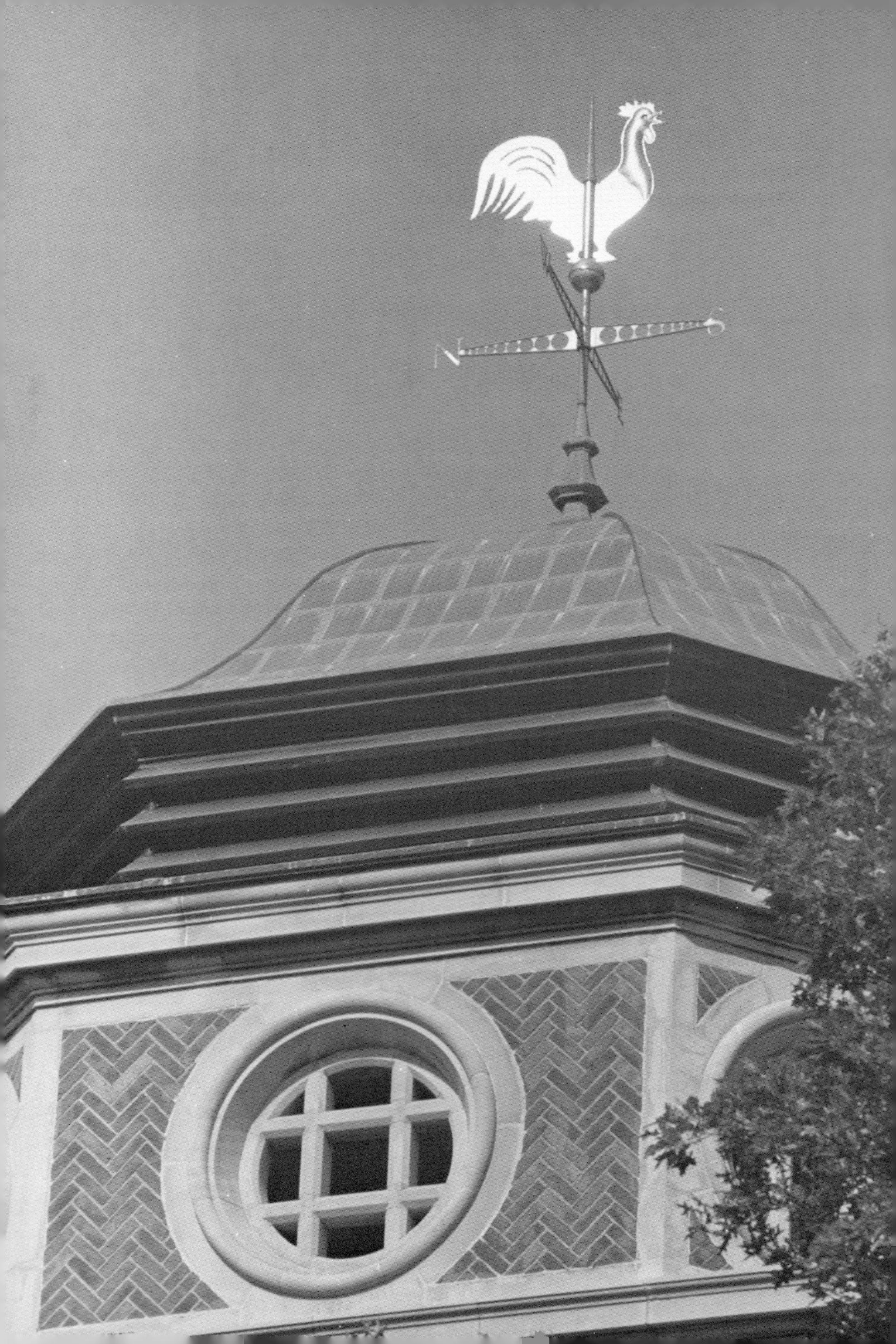
N
S

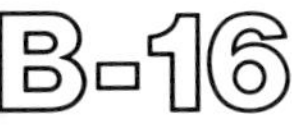

B. Wathof and Son

ROOSTER WEATHERVANE

1957, gilded brass, c. 5′

Central Reformed Church
College N.E. and E. Fulton, Grand Rapids

The rooster weathervane, placed on the roof of the Central Reformed Church on April 5, 1957, two days before the first service was held in the new building, was a gift of Mr. and Mrs. Robert J. Hemkes. The church was designed by Eggers and Higgins of New York in association with Daverman Associates of Grand Rapids. The placement of a rooster on the top of a church was traditional with the Reformed Church in the Netherlands and was brought to America by Dutch settlers in the seventeenth century. The tradition has been kept alive by the descendants of the Dutch settlers who came to Grand Rapids in the 1840s. This particular weathervane was made in Goor, Holland, by a firm which has made weathervanes for several generations. The rooster or chanticleer, who crows at the light of dawn to signal the beginning of a new day, symbolizes Christ's triumph over dark, evil, and death. The rooster also refers to the denial and repentenance of Peter who denied Christ three times before the cock crowed. This vigilant rooster becomes a literal symbol of light with his brilliant gold covering.

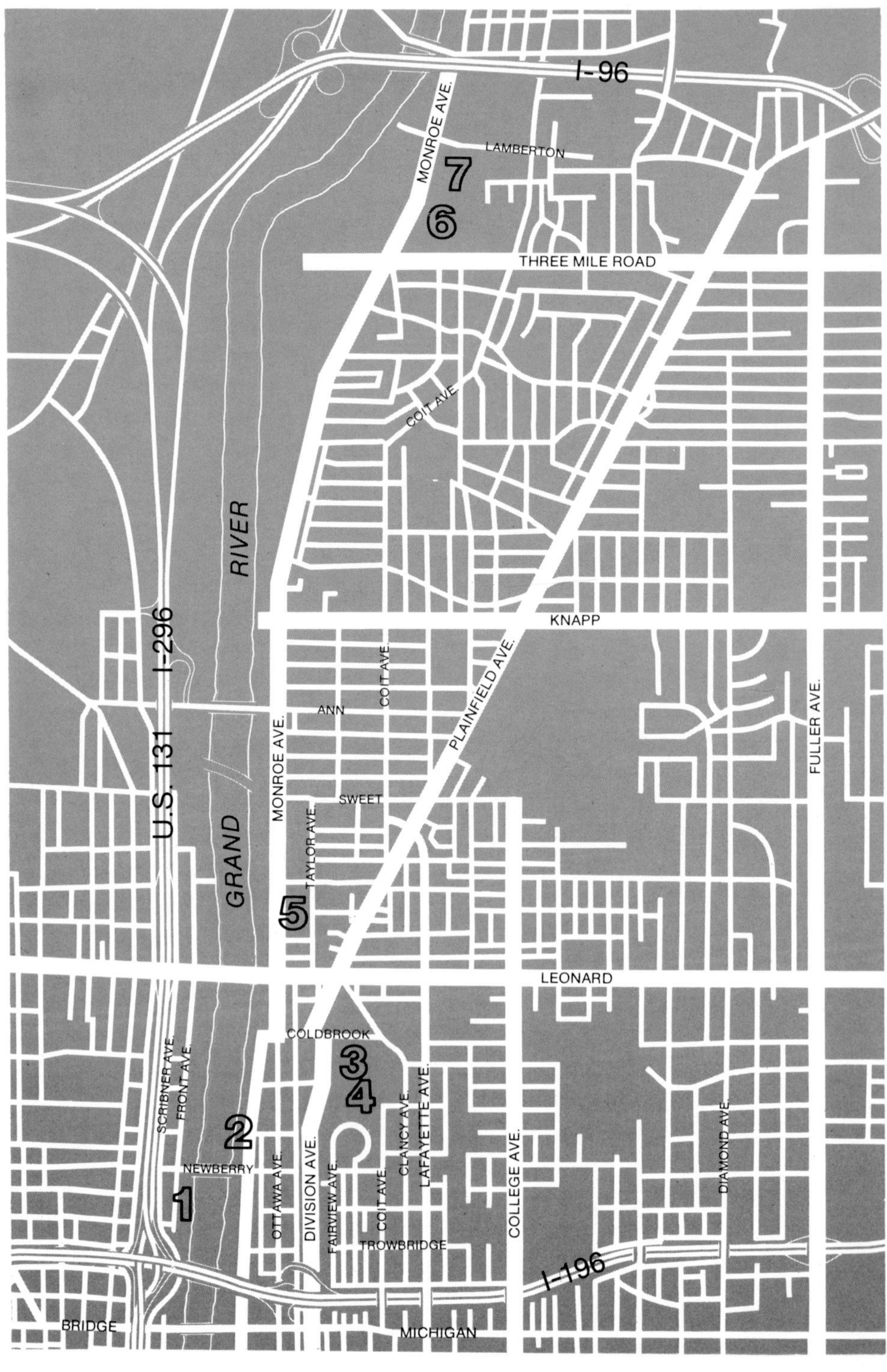

I-96
MONROE AVE.
LAMBERTON
7
6
THREE MILE ROAD
COIT AVE.
RIVER
KNAPP
I-296
PLAINFIELD AVE.
COIT AVE.
ANN
U.S. 131
MONROE AVE.
FULLER AVE.
SWEET
GRAND
TAYLOR AVE.
5
LEONARD
COLDBROOK
3
4
SCRIBNER AVE.
FRONT AVE.
2
CLANCY AVE.
LAFAYETTE AVE.
DIAMOND AVE.
NEWBERRY
OTTAWA AVE.
DIVISION AVE.
FAIRVIEW AVE.
COIT AVE.
COLLEGE AVE.
1
TROWBRIDGE
I-196
BRIDGE
MICHIGAN

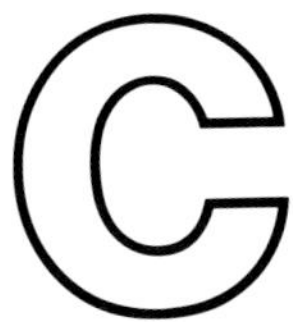

NORTH

1. Joseph E. Kinnebrew IV, GRAND RIVER SCULPTURE AND FISH LADDER

2. Joseph E. Kinnebrew IV, KID KATWALK
   Sixth Street Bridge Park

3. Horace F. Colby, CAPTAIN CHARLES E. BELKNAP
   Belknap Park

4. Robert Morris, GRAND RAPIDS PROJECT ("X")
   Belknap Park

5. Artist Unknown, CITY SEAL AND AQUARIUS RELIEFS
   Filter Plant

6. Artist Unknown, FOUNTAIN
   Michigan Veterans' Facility

7. Artist Unknown, SOLDIERS' MONUMENT
   Michigan Veterans' Facility

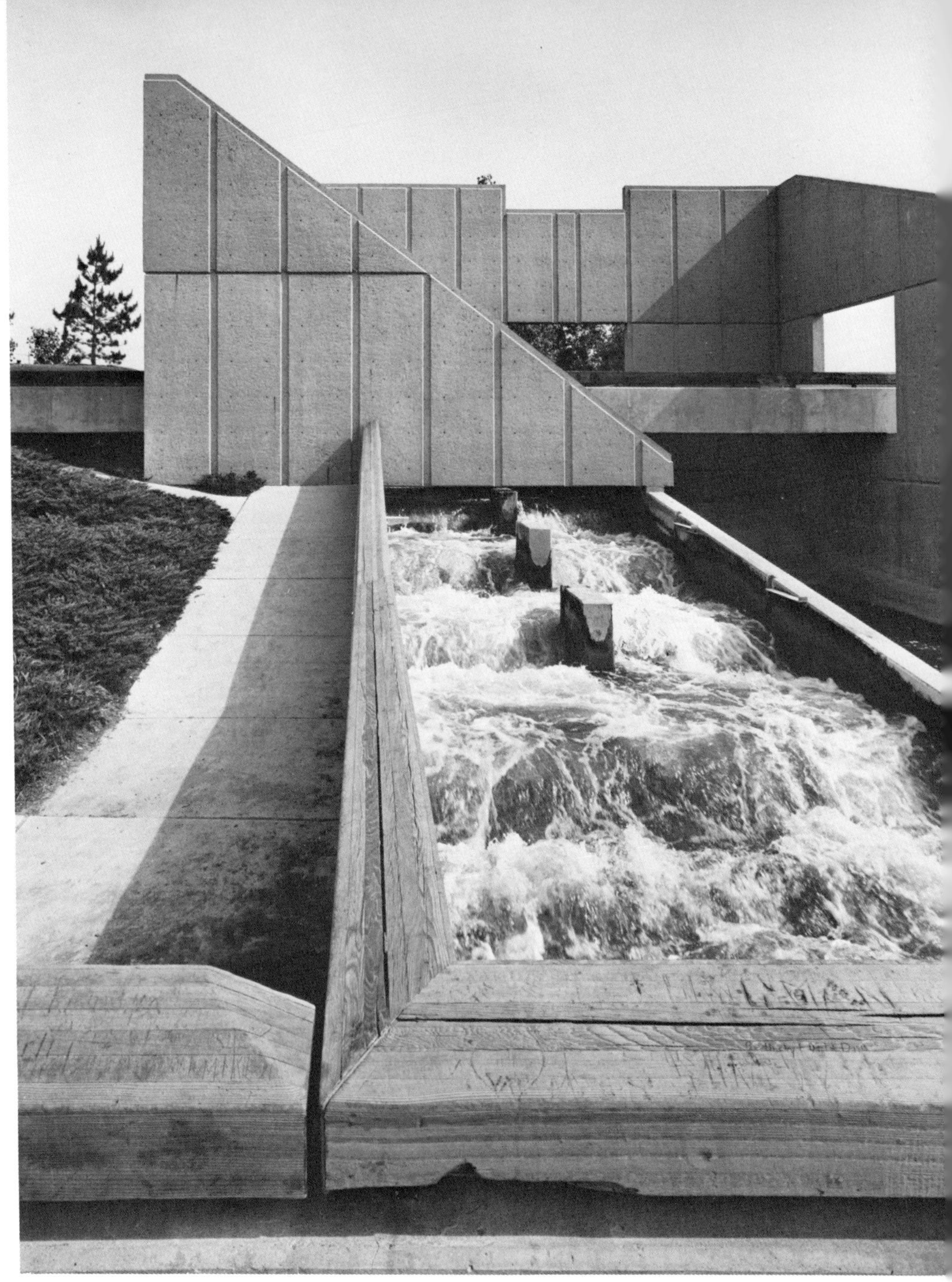

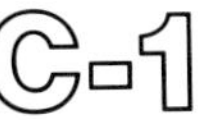

Joseph E. Kinnebrew IV (1942-   )

GRAND RIVER SCULPTURE AND FISH LADDER

1974, concrete, 34′

Front and Fourth Streets N.W., Grand Rapids

When the Michigan Department of Natural Resources suggested that a fish ladder be built to aid spawning fish in their swim upstream, Joseph Kinnebrew suggested that a superstructure be constructed over the ladder to allow people to interact with the fish and the water. The Department of Natural Resources provided the funds for the ladder and monies for the environmental sculpture were provided by Associated Truck Lines Foundation, Dexter Industries Charitable Trust, Dyer-Ives Foundation, Grand Rapids Foundation, the Michigan Council for the Arts, the National Endowment for the Arts, and the Thomas Erler Seidman Foundation. This theatrical stage is composed of textured geometric forms that fold around the fish ladder. *The Grand River Sculpture and Fish Ladder,* dedicated on June 6, 1975, as "a statement of the aesthetic significance of our environment," is one of the recent efforts to make the riverfront in Grand Rapids a focal point for people.

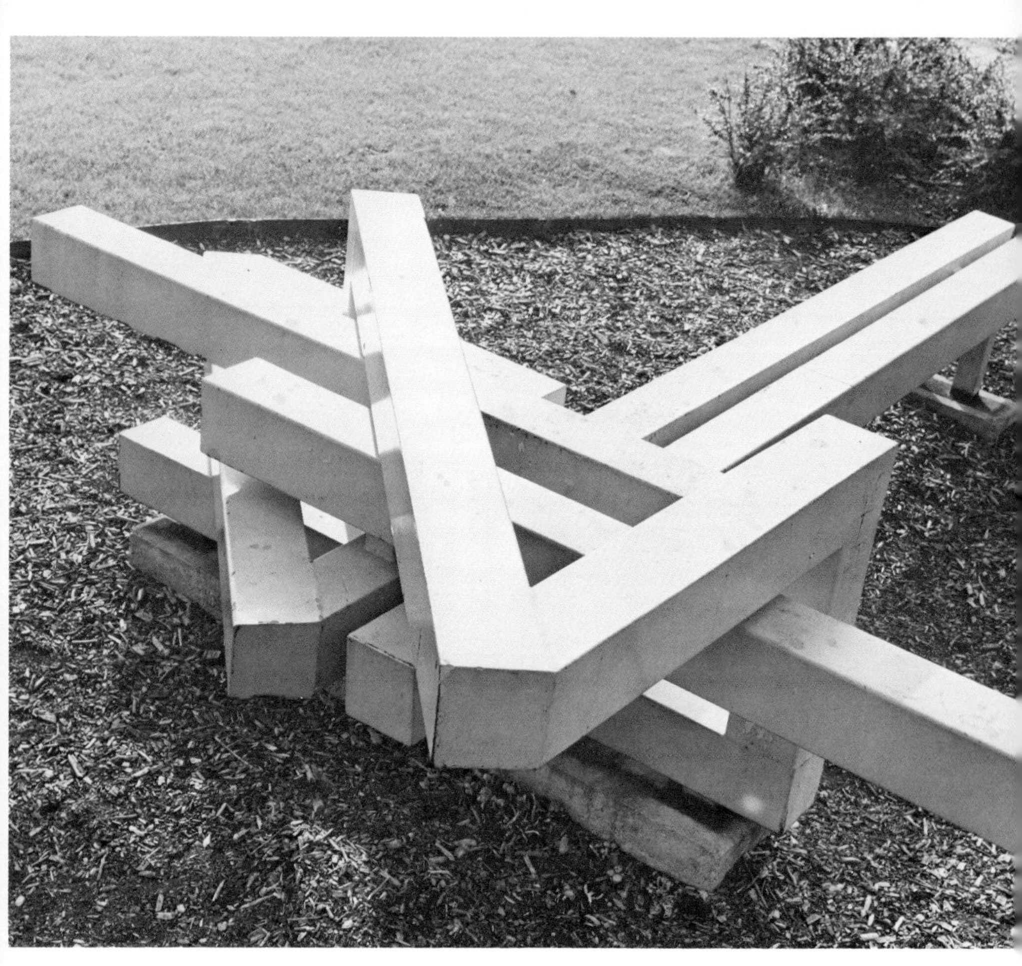

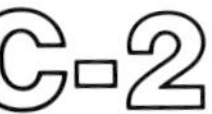

Joseph E. Kinnebrew IV (1942-   )

KID KATWALK

1975, steel, 3′6″

[Kinnebrew]

Sixth Street Bridge Park
647 Monroe N.W., Grand Rapids

Kid Katwalk was commissioned by Festival '75 for children to play on during the annual arts celebration in Grand Rapids. After Festival, it was permanently placed in the Sixth Street Bridge Park. This playground sculpture is composed of yellow cantilevered beams which form linear patterns. It provides a challenge to children as they balance their way along the narrow catwalks.

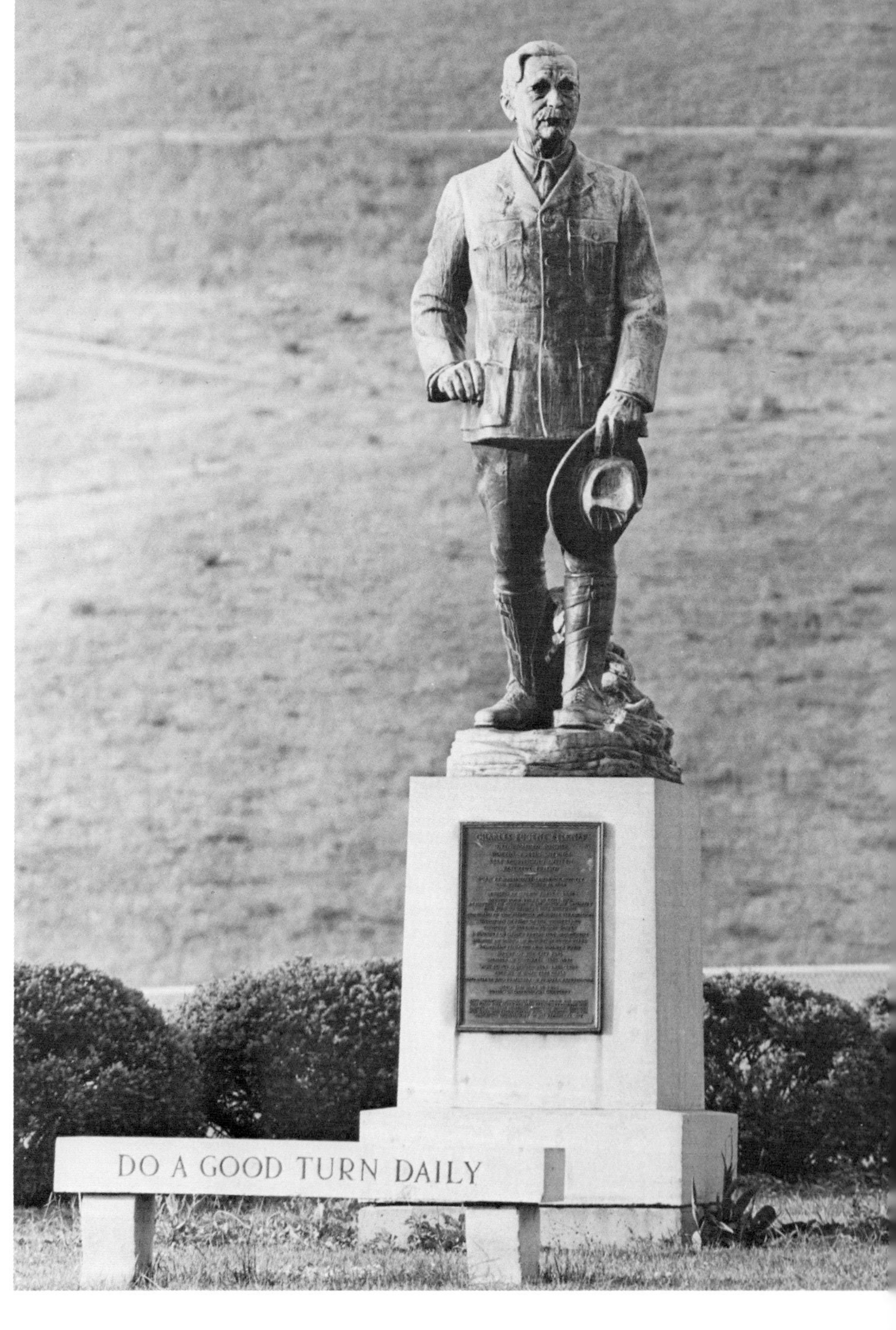
DO A GOOD TURN DAILY

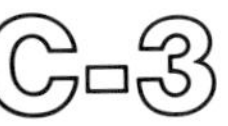

Horace F. Colby (1901-1966)

CAPTAIN CHARLES E. BELKNAP

1931, bronze, 8′6″

[Horace Colby Sc 1931]

Belknap Memorial Park
Coldbrook and Plainfield N.E., Grand Rapids

Even before the death of Captain Belknap (1846-1929), there was a move to erect a monument to this prominent citizen. Though the monument was inspired by the Boy Scouts and Camp Fire Girls, funds were provided by the whole community. The statue, cast at the Roman Bronze Works in New York and dedicated on December 26, 1931, was temporarily located in Baldwin Park at Lake Drive and E. Fulton. It was not until 1975 that the city was reminded of this temporary location and Belknap was moved to the park which also memorializes him. Belknap, who served in the Civil War, was founder of the Belknap Wagon and Sleigh Works. He also served in the fire department, as an alderman and mayor, and in the United States Congress. At the time of his death he was Commissioner for the Boy Scouts, whose uniform he wears. Belknap, a local historian and writer, was author of *The Yesterdays of Grand Rapids.*

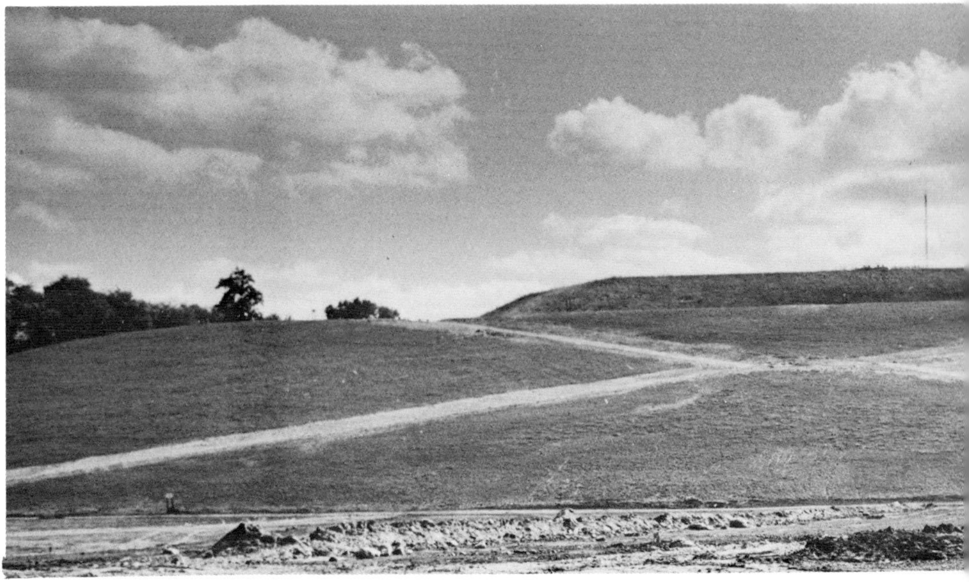

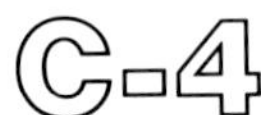

Robert Morris (1931-)

GRAND RAPIDS PROJECT ("X")

1974, earth and asphalt, 90′

Belknap Memorial Park
Coldbrook and Plainfield N.E., Grand Rapids

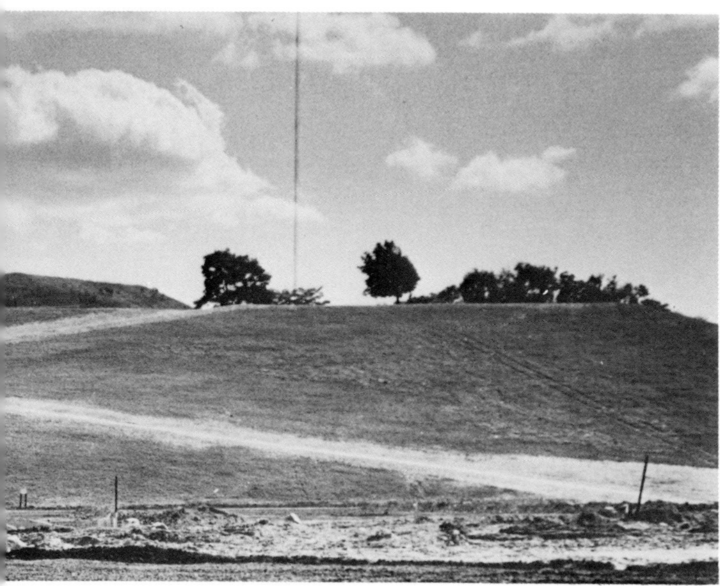

PHOTO: Craig Vander Lende

Around 1960 plans were made to remove the hill in Belknap Park for construction of U.S. 131 and to further develop the recreational facilities at the park. However, only part of the hill was removed and the completion of the park was left in limbo for several years. In 1973 Robert Morris offered a solution to this scarred hillside with his plans for the *Grand Rapids Project,* which were included in the exhibition *Sculpture Off the Pedestal.* The Women's Committee of the Grand Rapids Art Museum commissioned the environmental work which was dedicated on October 19, 1974. Funds for the "X" were provided by the National Endowment for the Arts, the Michigan Council for the Arts, the Women's Committee, and the city of Grand Rapids. The earthwork was Morris' first to be constructed in the United States. It consists of a sculptural form which was carved out of the earth and articulated by two intersecting asphalt pathways. The only way to comprehend the environmental work is to walk through, above, and below it. The form, which changes with the viewpoint, also changes with the light and the seasons.

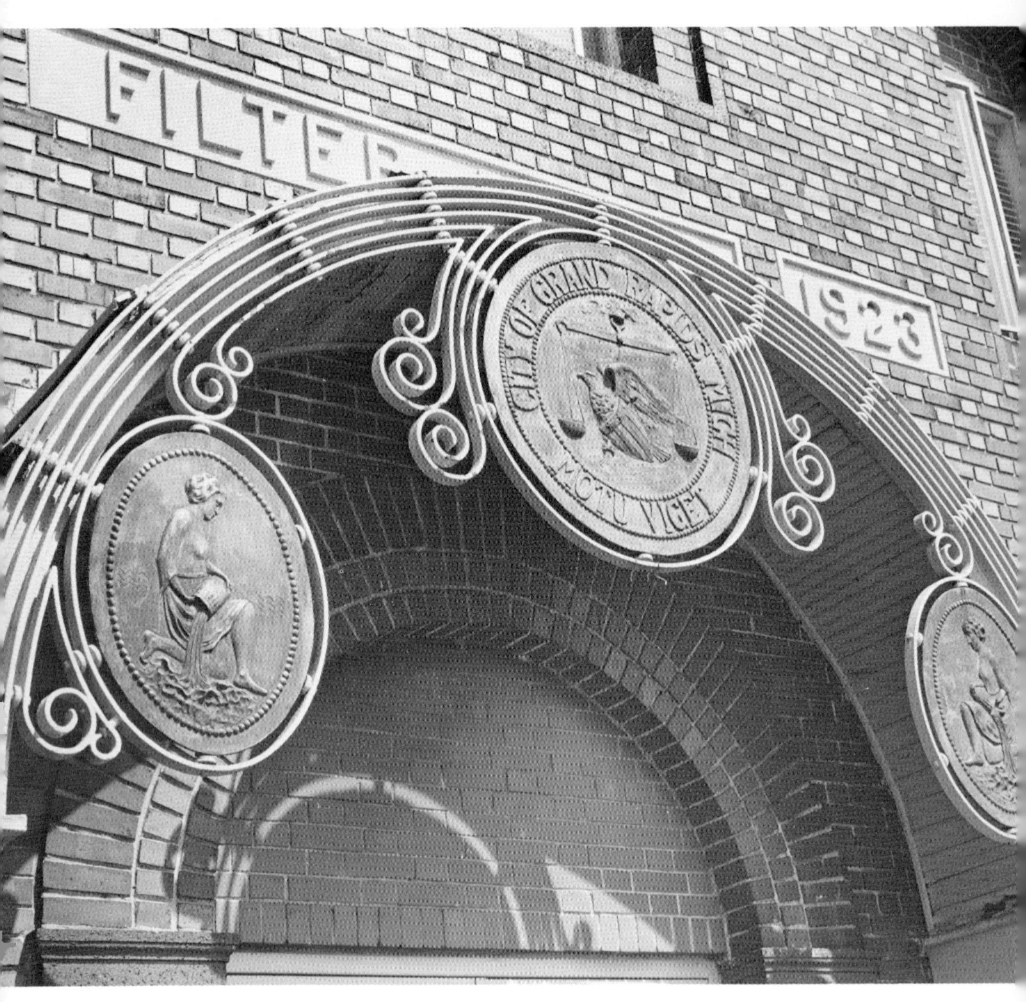
FILTER
1923
CITY OF GRAND RAPIDS MICH
MOTU VIGET

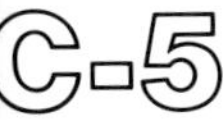

Artist Unknown

CITY SEAL AND AQUARIUS RELIEFS

c. 1912, bronze (?), seal 35", *Aquarius* 28"

Filter Plant
1430 Monroe N.W., Grand Rapids

On December 31, 1912, residents were urged to toast the new year with a glass of city water. The construction of the Filter Plant, designed by Hering and Fuller of New York, was a long awaited event which considerably reduced the incidence of typhoid fever in the city. Above the doorway the city seal is flanked by the maiden *Aquarius.* The city seal was designed by Aaron B. Turner, city clerk, when Grand Rapids passed from a village to a city in 1850. The seal portrays a hand reaching down from the clouds and holding the scales of justice. An American eagle, with arrows at its feet, is protected by a shield which bears three stars, one each for city, state, and nation. The motto, *Motu Viget,* is taken from Vergil, and freely translated, means "strength through activity."

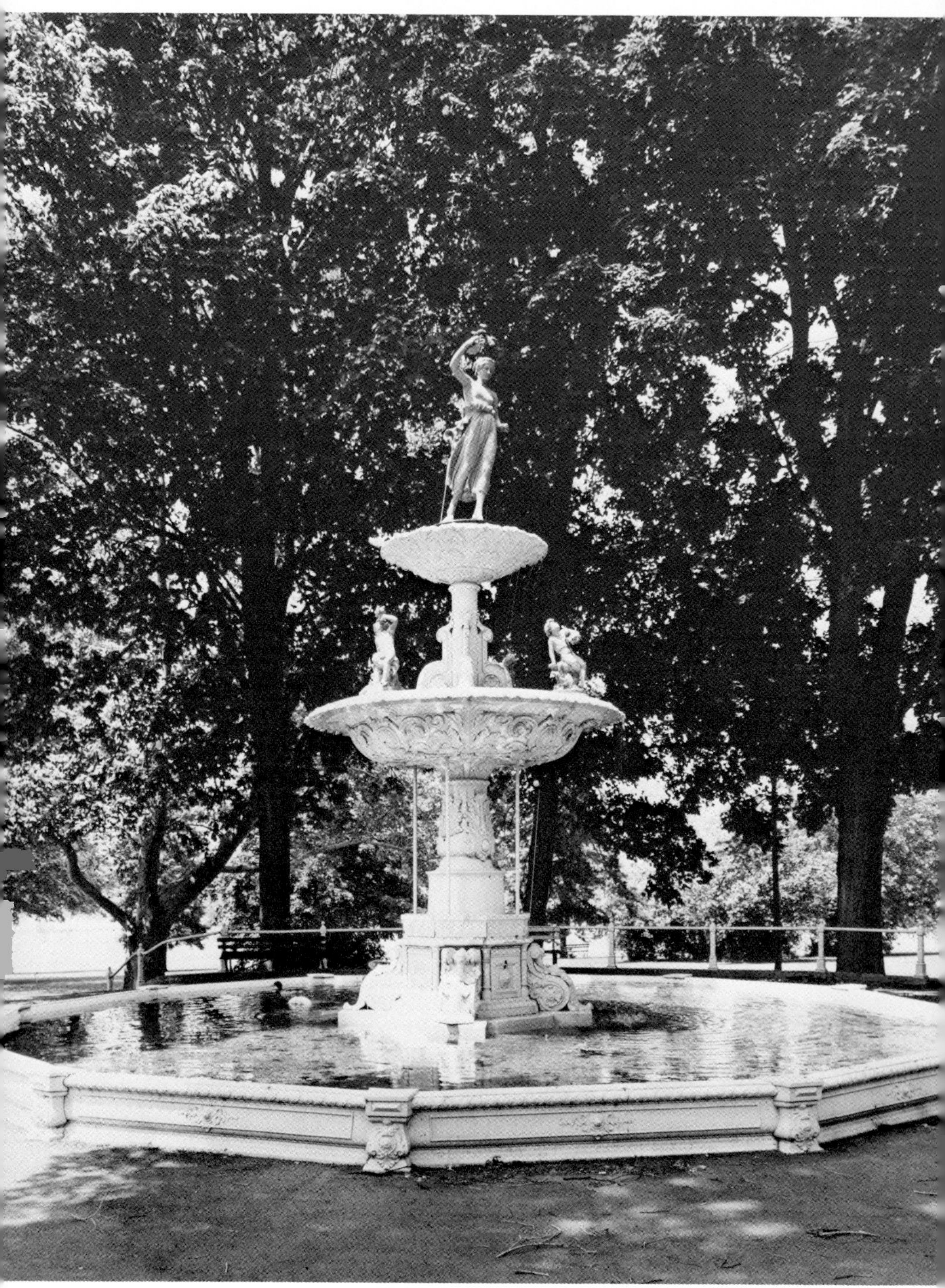

C-6

Artist Unknown

FOUNTAIN

c. 1893, cast iron, c. 22′

[J. L. Mott, N.Y.]

Michigan Veterans' Facility (Soldiers' Home)
3000 Monroe N.W., Grand Rapids

The Soldiers' Home, dedicated on December 30, 1886, was erected for Michigan soldiers who had fought in the Civil War. In the fourth biennial Report of the Board of Managers, ending June 30, 1892, there was a suggestion that some attempt at ornamentation be made to relieve the monotonous appearance of the grounds. By the next report, ending June 30, 1894, this Victorian fountain had been ordered from J. L. Mott Iron Works in New York and placed in front of the building. Funds may have been provided by the posthumous fund which derived its monies from deceased veterans at the Soldiers' Home. Based on a watery theme, the young woman at the top pours water from a pitcher while the youths below drink water from a shell. Swans and children were originally located near the base of the fountain. When "Old Main," as the Soldiers' Home came to be called, was scheduled to be torn down to make way for a new building, the fountain was scheduled to go as well. However, plans were changed and the fountain was restored. It was rededicated by the United Veterans Council on October 8, 1972.

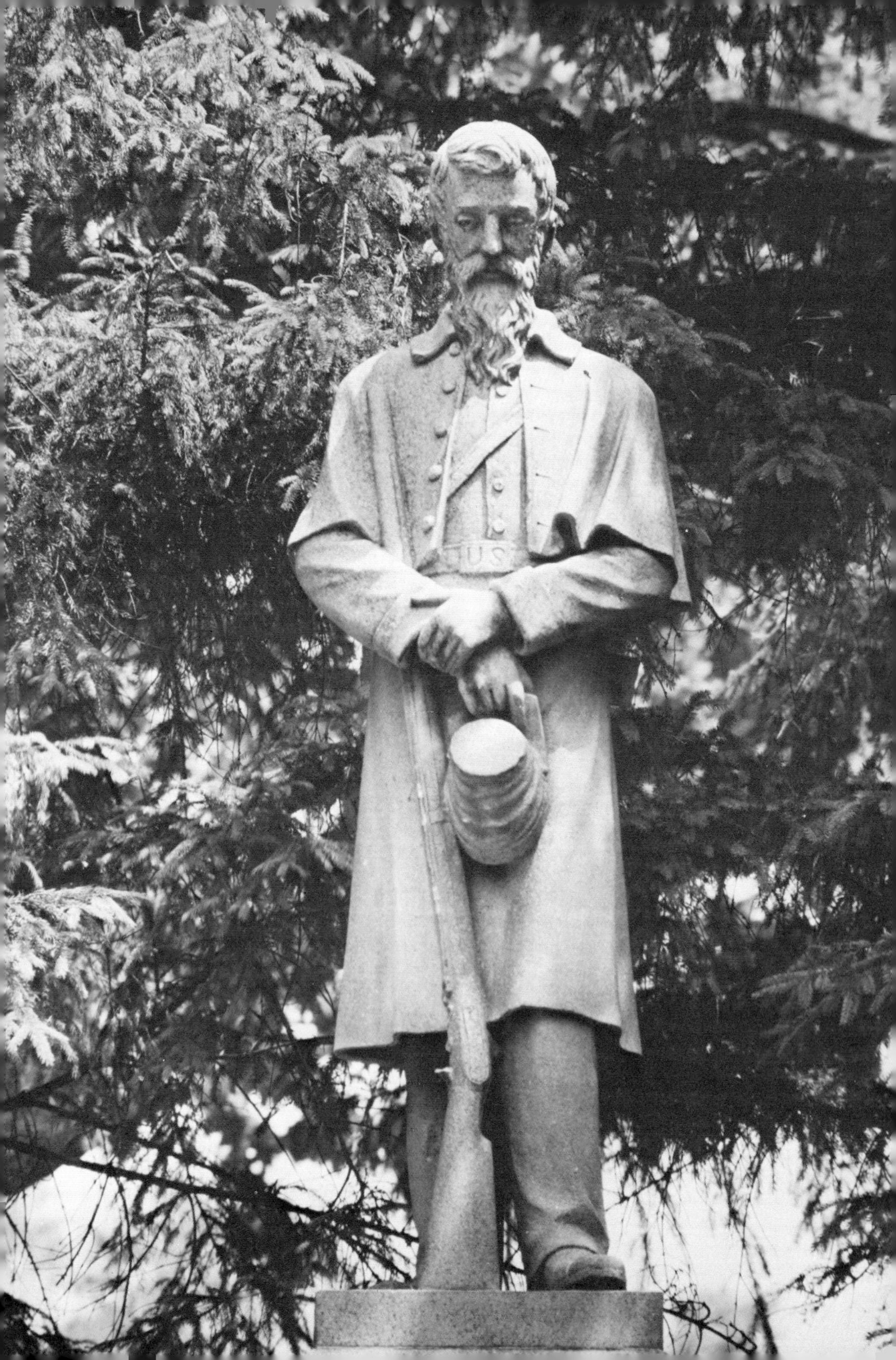
US

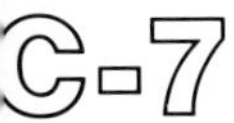

Artist Unknown

SOLDIERS' MONUMENT

c. 1893, granite, c. 9′

Cemetery, Michigan Veterans' Facility (Soldiers' Home)
3000 Monroe N.W., Grand Rapids

When the Soldiers' Home was constructed in 1886, a cemetery was laid out on the grounds in the form of a maltese cross and dedicated on May 31 of that same year. A few years later a monument was erected in the cemetery with funds provided by the sale of garbage and from monies left by deceased veterans from the Soldiers' Home. One can only presume that the garbage was sold to a piggery. This lone soldier, who stands for the many, has removed his hat and stands at rest. Though this type of memorial with a soldier on a high pedestal was popular after the Civil War, each is quite often an individualized monument.

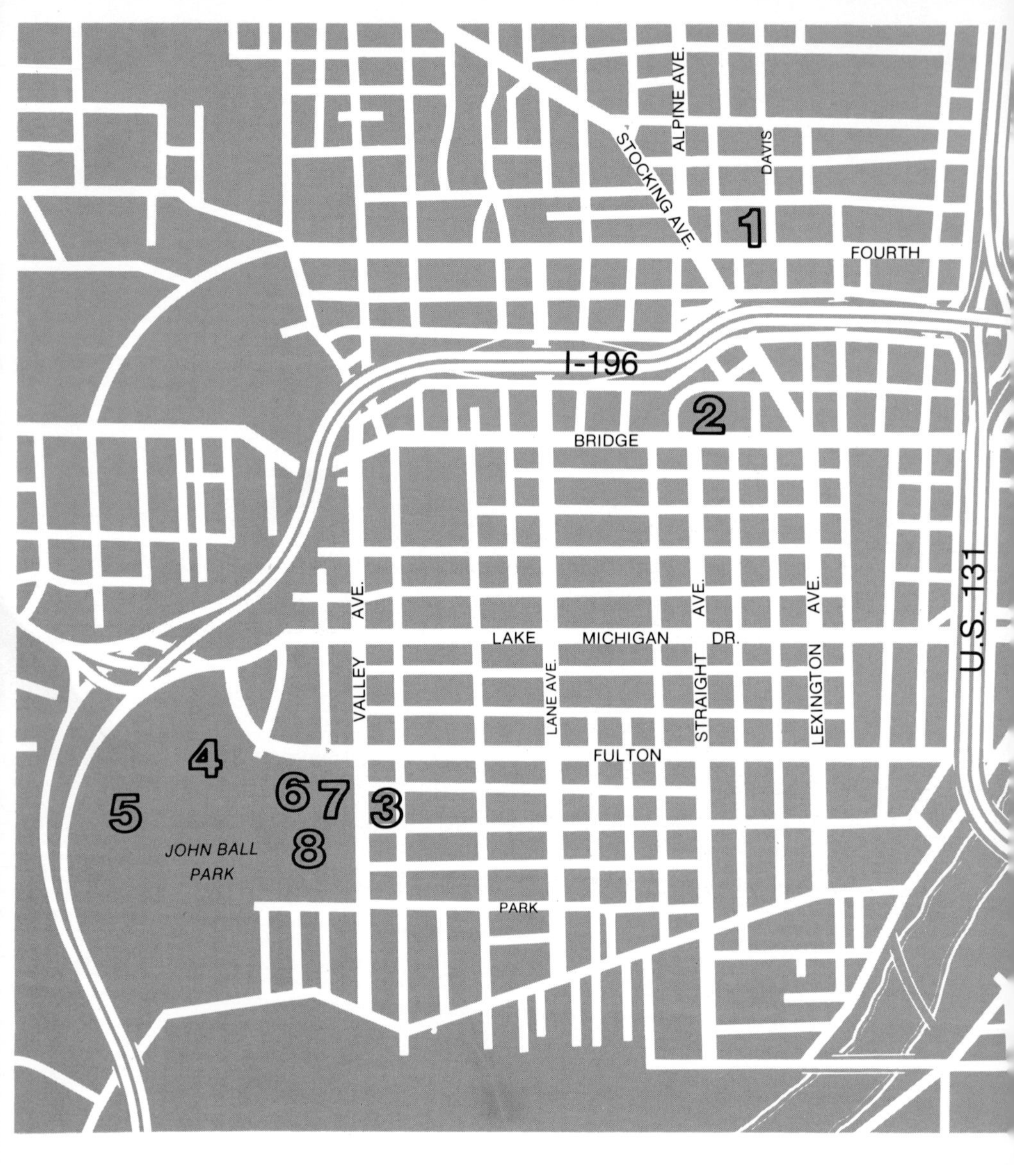

ALPINE AVE.
STOCKING AVE.
DAVIS
1
FOURTH
I-196
2
BRIDGE
VALLEY AVE.
LAKE MICHIGAN DR.
LANE AVE.
STRAIGHT AVE.
LEXINGTON AVE.
U.S. 131
FULTON
4
5
6
7
3
8
JOHN BALL PARK
PARK

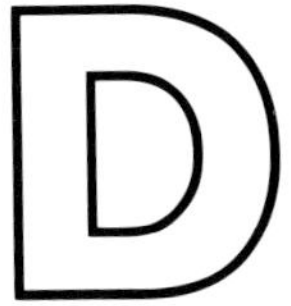

WEST

1. Attilio D. and Paola M. Gandola, ANGELS WITH GOLDEN TRUMPETS
   Saint Adalbert Church

2. Artist Unknown, SAINT JAMES (?),
   Saint James Church

3. Artist Unknown, NATIVITY, CRUCIFIXION, ASCENSION
   Sacred Heart Church

4. Pompeo L. Coppini, JOHN BALL MEMORIAL
   John Ball Memorial Park

5. Artist Unknown, SUNDIAL
   John Ball Memorial Park

6. Robert A. Jensen, EARTH LOOPS
   John Ball Memorial Park

7. Robbin L. Crawford, ORANGE-GANIC DOMINO
   John Ball Memorial Park

8. Mary Gardner Preminger, RECREFORM
   John Ball Memorial Park

Attilio D. Gandola (1884-1930)

Paola M. Gandola (1889-1963)

ANGELS WITH GOLDEN TRUMPETS

c. 1910, limestone (?), c. 11′

Saint Adalbert Church
644 Davis N.W., Grand Rapids

In 1880 the Polish community of Grand Rapids met to form a new parish which was named after Saint Adalbert. Many of them had come from Trzemeszno where their former parish church was also dedicated to the saint. Trzemeszno is located near Gnessen where the martyred Saint Adalbert was buried. Saint Adalbert (939-997) was Bishop of Prague and helped to evangelize central Europe, including present day Poland. In 1907 the cornerstone was laid for a new church which was designed by Cleveland architect Henry J. Harks. By 1910 the angels were carved and in place and the church was consecrated on June 22, 1913. The four angles with golden trumpets, which surround the dome of heaven, stand at the four corners of the earth ready to blow their trumpets on Judgement Day. Though no specific angels are mentioned in Revelations 7:1, these four may represent archangels sounding their trumpets.

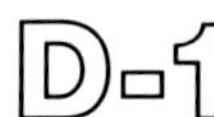

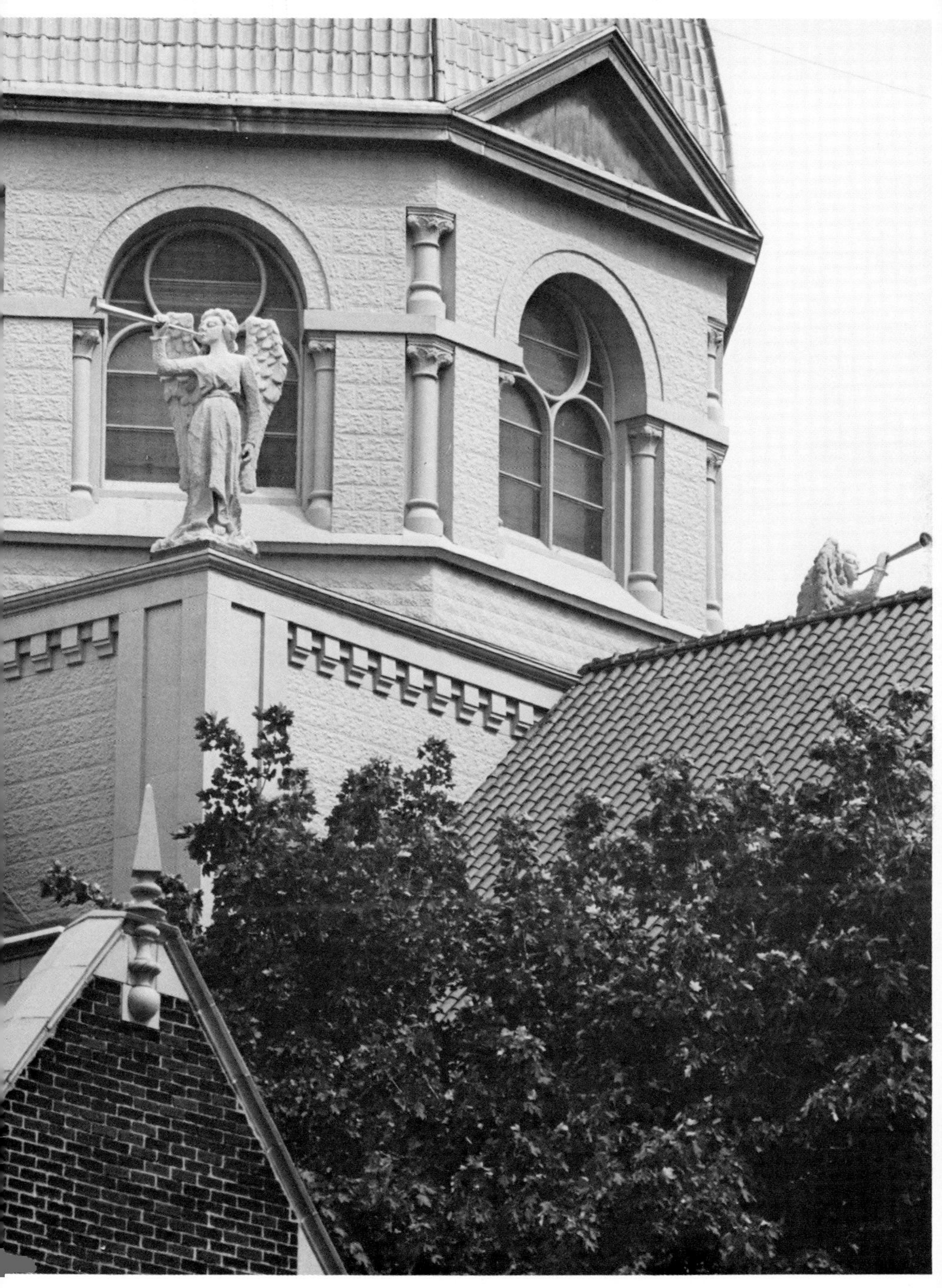

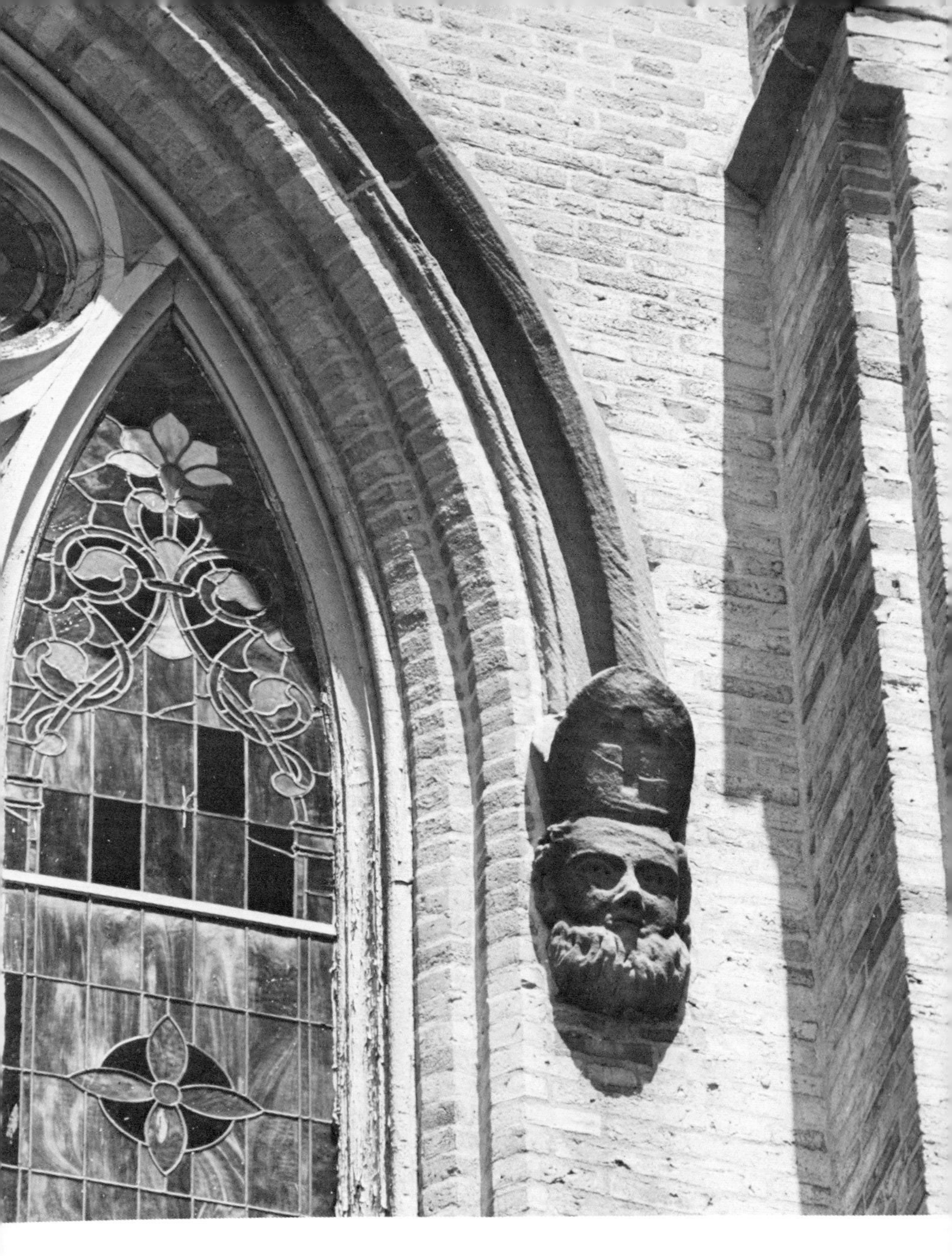

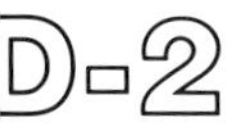

Artist Unknown

SAINT JAMES (?)

c. 1872, sandstone, c. 2′

Saint James Church
733 Bridge N.W., Grand Rapids

Saint James Church was designed by Grand Rapids architect William G. Robinson (1835-1907) and dedicated in July of 1872. Saint James Parish, daughter parish of Saint Andrew, was founded shortly before the dedication and was composed primarily of Irish families. The parish was named in honor of the patron saint of the first pastor, Father James C. Pulcher. Saint James the Greater was a martyred Apostle who is said to have been the first archbishop of Spain. Perhaps it is the roughly carved and weathered images of Saint James that can be found on the facade of the church. Two heads of a balding and bearded man can be found at the base of the Gothic molding over the doorway. Two more heads of a bearded man wearing a mitre can be found at the base of similar molding which surrounds the stained glass window above the doorway.

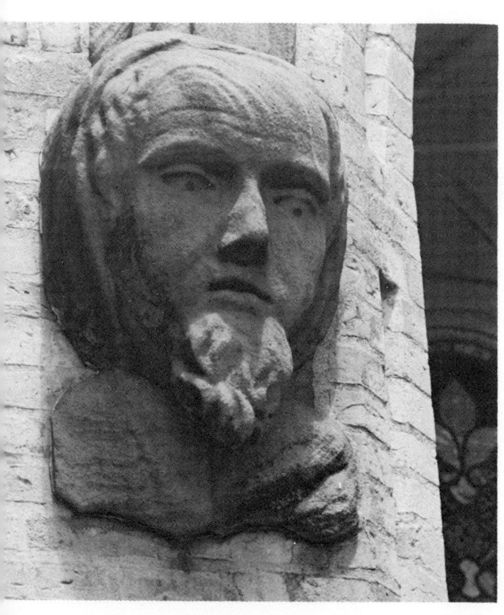

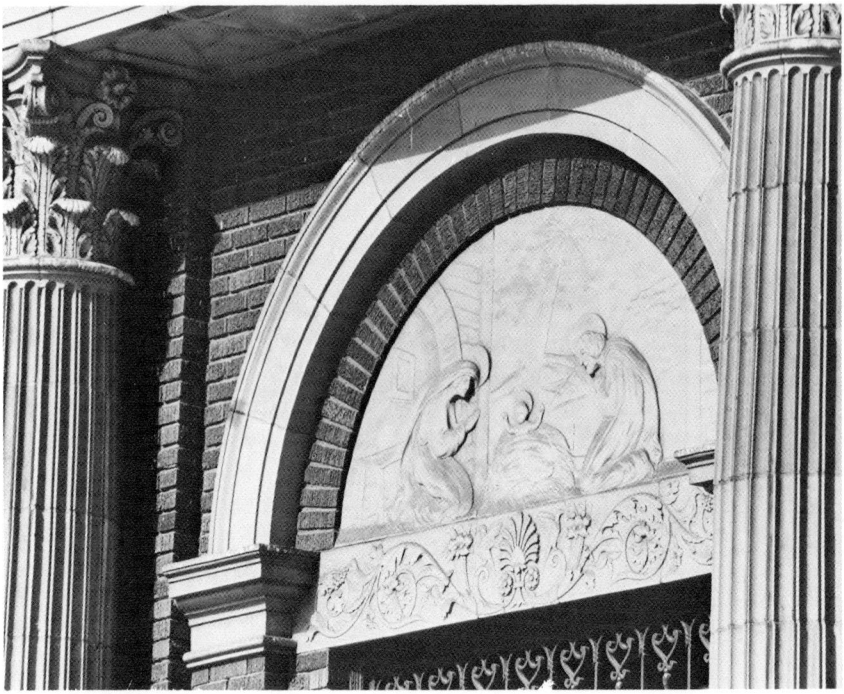

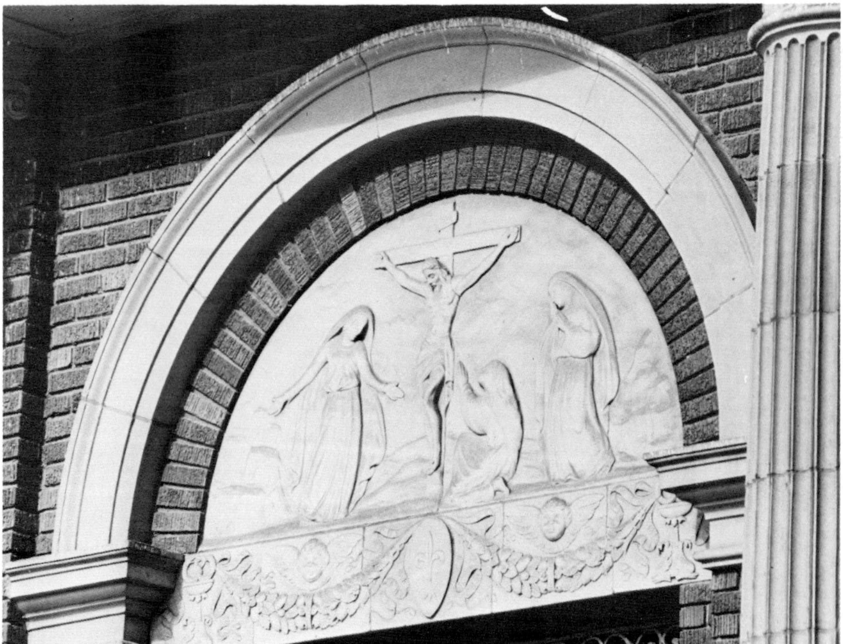

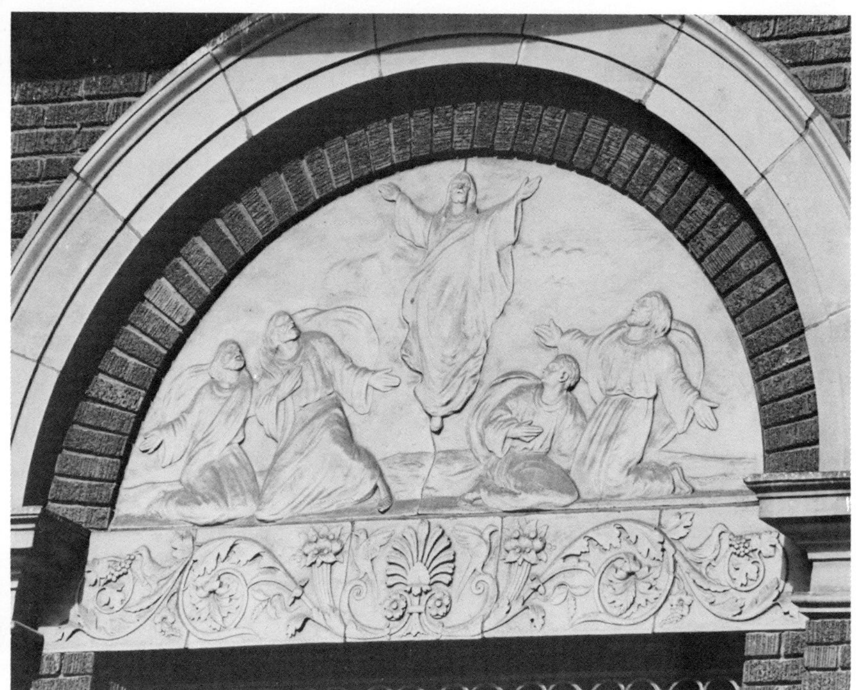

D-3

Artist Unknown

NATIVITY, CRUCIFIXION, ASCENSION

c. 1922, terra cotta (?), c. 4′

Sacred Heart Church
151 Garfield S.W., Grand Rapids

Sacred Heart Church, designed by Brillmeier & Co. of Milwaukee, was dedicated on New Year's Day of 1924. Sacred Heart Parish, daughter parish of Saint Adalbert, was founded in 1903 to meet the needs of the Polish families in the southwestern part of Grand Rapids. The tympanum above each of the doorways to the church contains a scene from the life of Christ. From left to right the scenes portray Christ's birth, His death, and His ascension into heaven.

Pompeo L. Coppini (1870-1957)

JOHN BALL MEMORIAL

1925, bronze, 6'5"

[P. Coppini Sc 1925]

John Ball Memorial Park
Valley N.W. and W. Fulton, Grand Rapids

John Ball (1794-1884), an adventurous world traveler who often kept accounts of his trips, came to Grand Rapids in 1836 as a land speculator. A lawyer and school teacher, Ball also served on the Board of Education and as a state legislator. When he died, Ball left forty acres which became the nucleus of the park and zoo which bear his name. Around the turn of the century, Theodore J. Wildberger, a fireman, carved a bust of Ball and proposed that the city have it cast in bronze. The city declined and did not commission a memorial until several years later. This grouping, dedicated on September 19, 1925, was based on a sketch by Mrs. Gertrude Van Houten. Pompeo Coppini also consulted photographs of Ball's grandson, Waldo M. Ball, and his great-grandchildren, Virginia and Albert Ellis Ball. Ball, who was beloved by children, continues to extend his love and his lap to the many children who keep this memorial well polished.

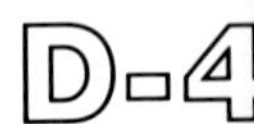

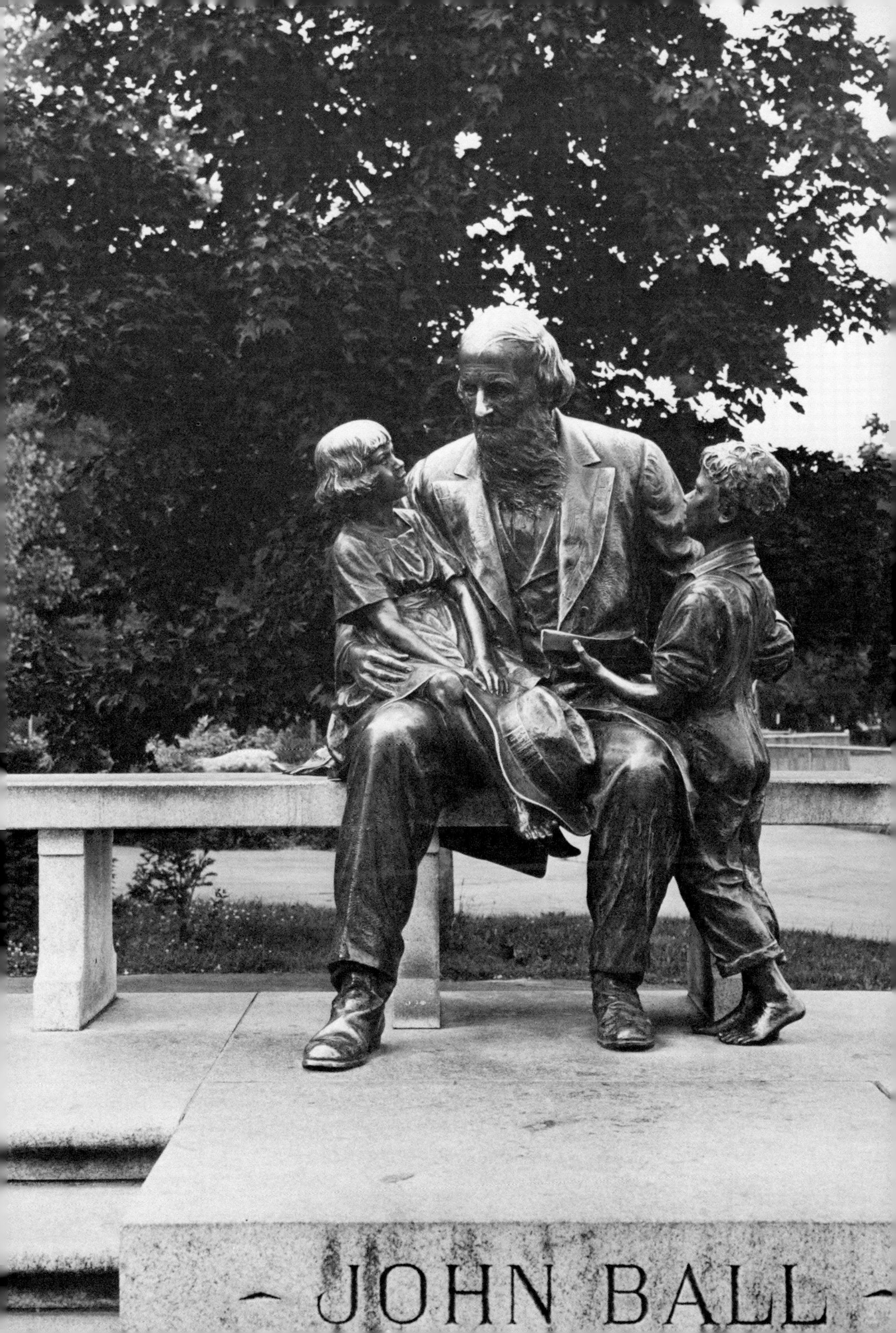
JOHN BALL

Artist Unkown

SUNDIAL

c. 1925, cast iron, 29′

John Ball Memorial Park Zoo
Valley N.W. and W. Fulton, Grand Rapids

In 1925 Mrs. Katherine Aldrich Blake gave the sundial and a portion of the Aldrich property to the city in memory of her father, Moses V. Aldrich (1829-1879). Aldrich, a businessman who came to Grand Rapids in 1855, expanded his business interests into the field of banking. He also served as mayor from 1869 to 1870 and County Superintendent of the Poor from 1875 until his death. The sundial, an ancient time-telling device, immensely popular in Europe, has been used in the United States primarily as a garden ornament. This graceful little sundial figure was originally the focal point of Sundial Park. The park is Grand Rapids' smallest park and is located at the northeast corner of College Avenue and Cherry Street. Around 1970 the sundial was painted gold and placed inside the zoo at John Ball Park. Though the motto on the sundial has become difficult to read, the little figure appears to be saying "I count none but sunny hours, fleeting time carelessly as the cupid in the golden world."

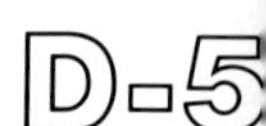

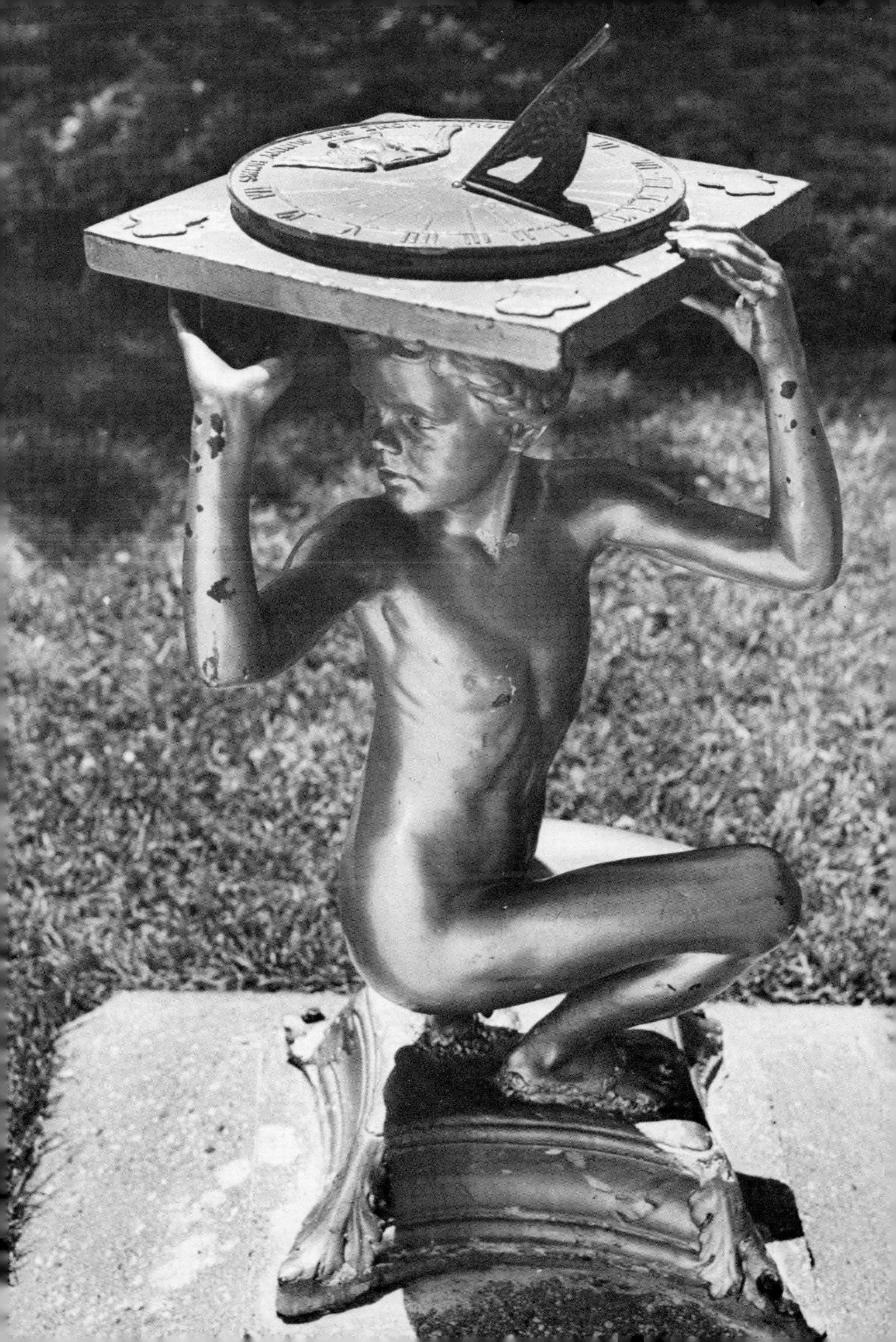

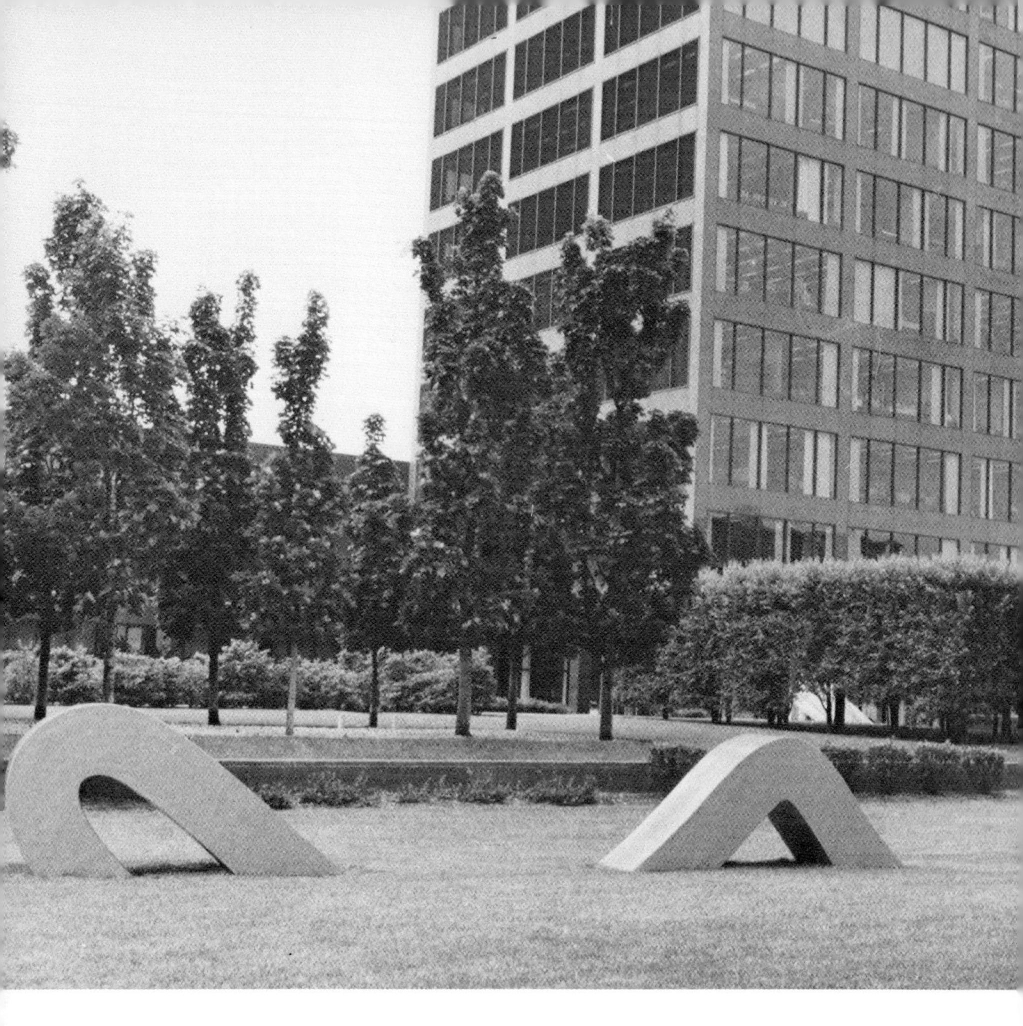

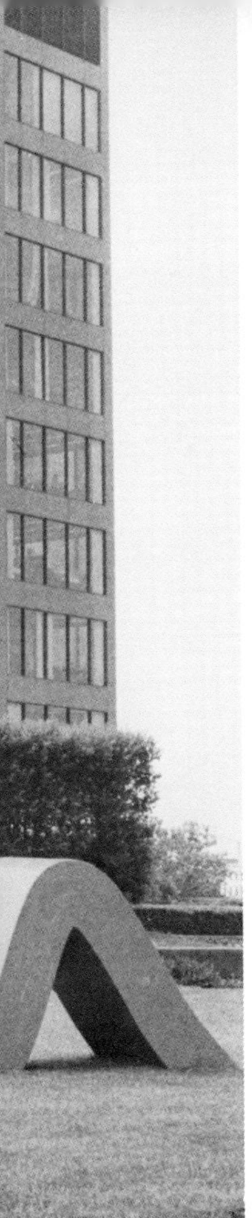

PHOTO: Fay L. Hendry

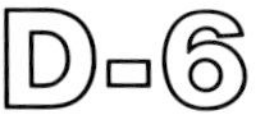

Robert A. (Robin) Jensen (1930-)

EARTH LOOPS

1978, epoxy resin and fiber glass over polystyrene core, 6′

[R Jensen]

John Ball Memorial Park
Valley N.W. and W. Fulton, Grand Rapids

Earth Loops, winner of the Playground Sculpture Competition for Festival '78, was created by Calvin College Art Professor Robin Jensen. Temporarily located on Calder Plaza for the art festival, it now has a permanent home in John Ball Park. This sculpture is composed of giant orange, yellow, and blue loops which snake their way in and out of the ground. As children slide and climb over the sculpture, they are able to experience a joyful human involvement with the earth. The sculpture is part of Jensen's *Jauntin'* series begun in 1977. For Jensen, jauntin' means an adventurous life journey filled with creativity which glorifies God.

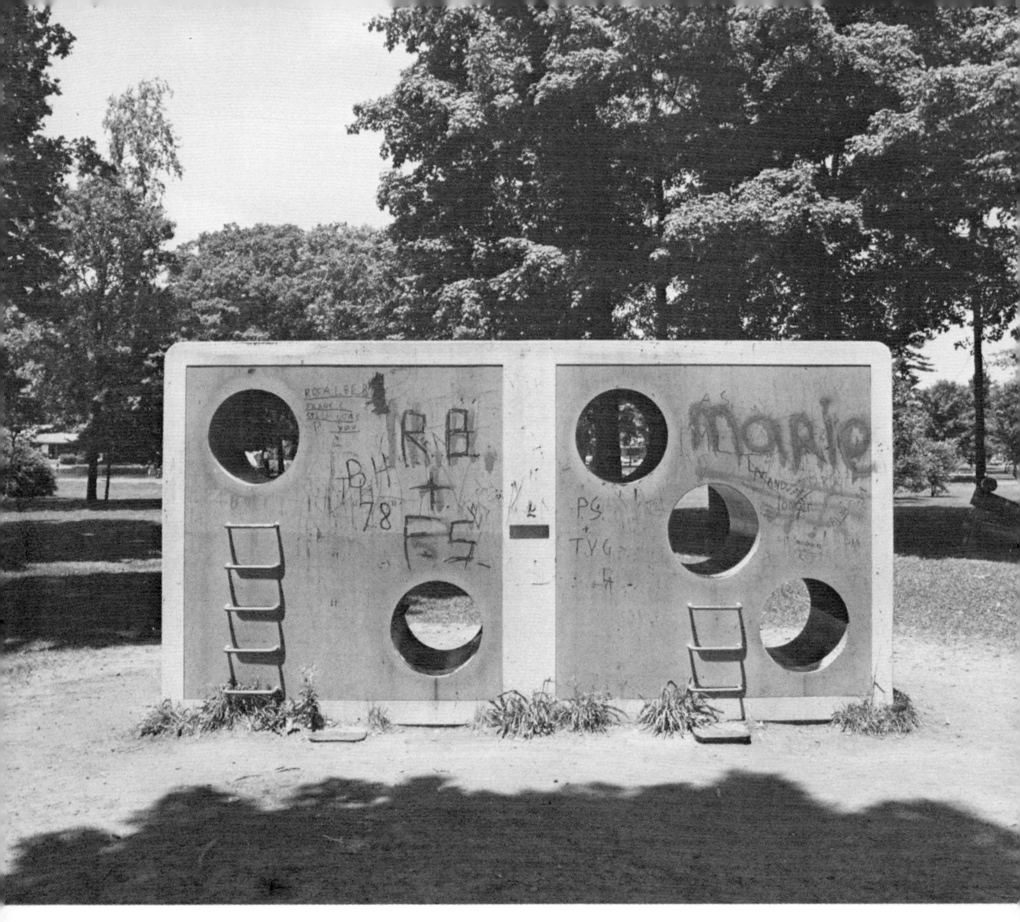
R.B
+
F.S
78"
P.S.
+
T.V.G
mario

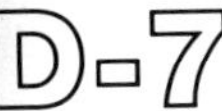

Robbin L. Crawford (1937-)

ORANGE-GANIC DOMINO

1977, steel, 7′

[R shaped like a robin]

John Ball Memorial Park
Valley N.W. and W. Fulton, Grand Rapids

This orange and yellow domino won the Playground Sculpture Competition for Festival '77 and was temporarily located on Calder Plaza. The five holes, which replace the traditional dots on a domino, encourage children to climb over and through the playground sculpture, while the large expanses of the domino invite graffiti. Both the gigantic size and orange color contribute to the playful title of this work.

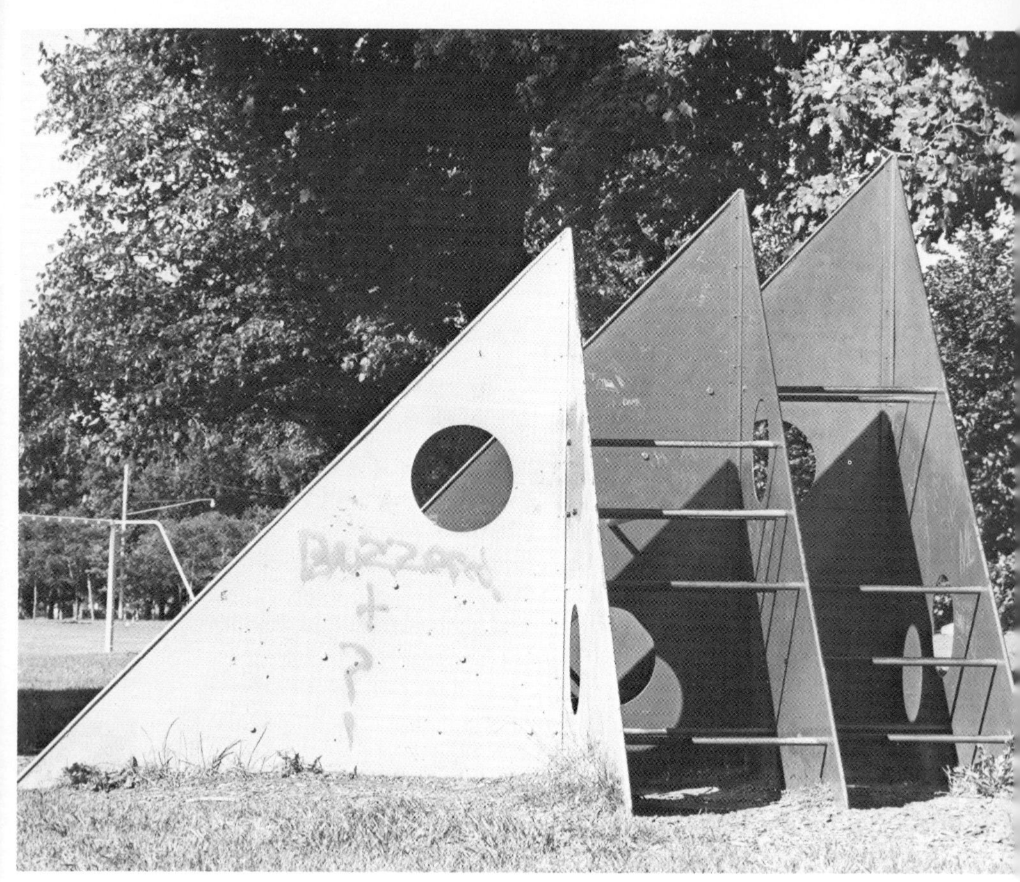

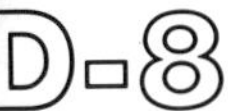

Mary Gardner Preminger (c. 1926-)

RECREFORM

1974, steel, 9′8″

John Ball Memorial Park
Valley N.W. and W. Fulton, Grand Rapids

This playground sculpture was created for Festival '74, Grand Rapids' annual art celebration which is held on Calder Plaza. It was a gift from the artist and was later moved to John Ball Park. This Recreform, the only one made of metal, is part of a series of architectonic sculpture that Mary Preminger has developed for parks, plazas, and shopping malls. The piece consists of three triangular forms of varying heights which are pierced by circles and joined together by rods. Children are invited to move in and out, up and down, and around these forms which are painted red, blue, and orange.

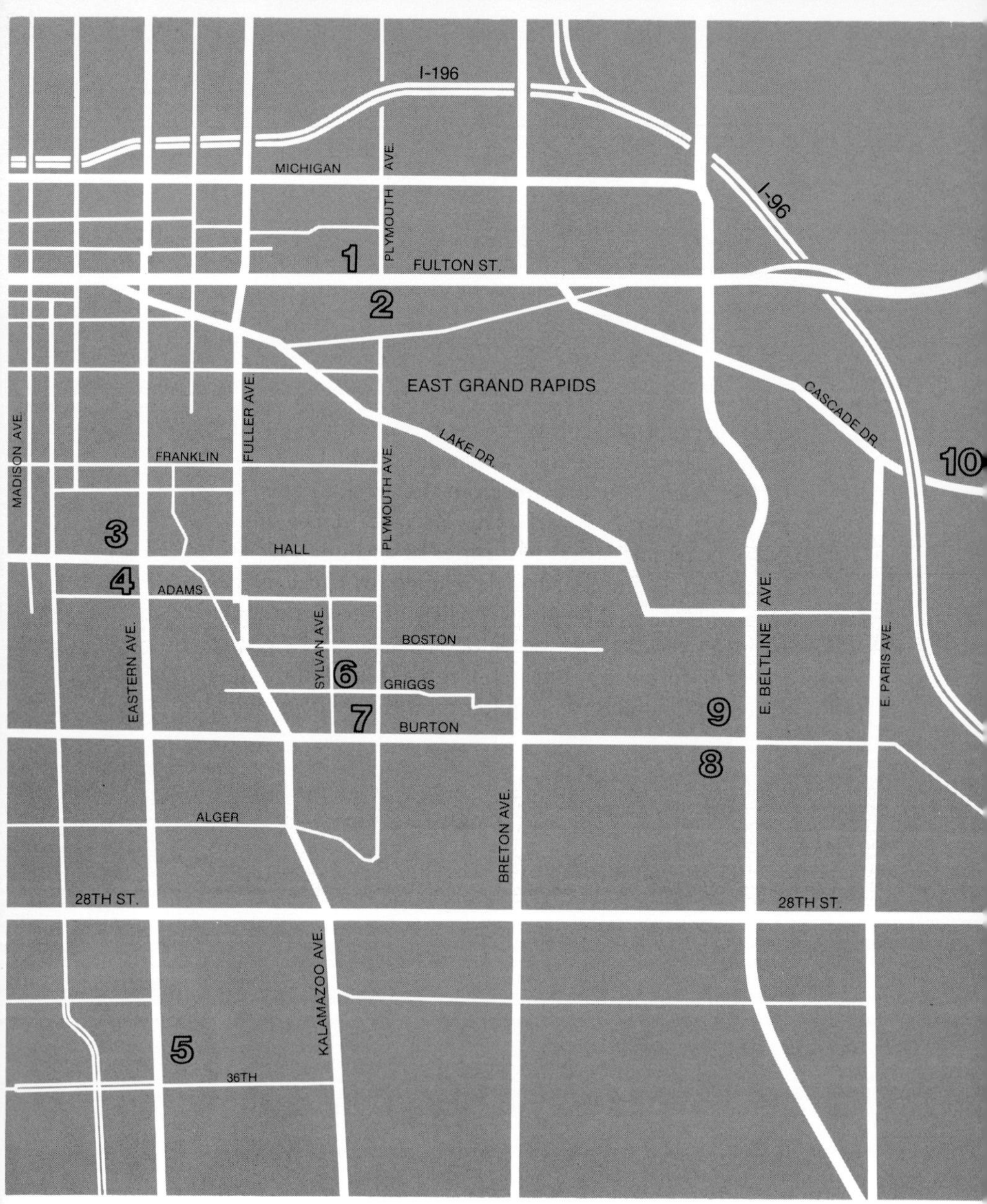
I-196
MICHIGAN
AVE.
I-96
PLYMOUTH
FULTON ST.
1
2
EAST GRAND RAPIDS
CASCADE DR.
LAKE DR.
10
MADISON AVE.
FRANKLIN
FULLER AVE.
PLYMOUTH AVE.
3
HALL
4
ADAMS
EASTERN AVE.
SYLVAN AVE.
BOSTON
6
GRIGGS
7
BURTON
9
8
E. BELTLINE AVE.
E. PARIS AVE.
ALGER
BRETON AVE.
28TH ST.
28TH ST.
KALAMAZOO AVE.
5
36TH

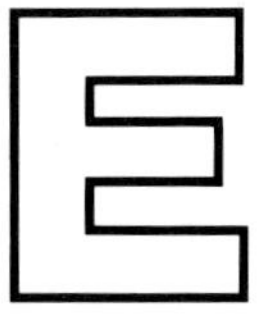

SOUTHEAST

1. Calvin Albert, BURNING BUSH
   Temple Emanuel

2. Artist Unknown, LIONS, URNS
   Saint Thomas Aquinas College

3. Artist Unknown, A. B. WATSON MAUSOLEUM
   Oak Hill Cemetery

4. Otto Vanselow, KENDALL MONUMENT
   Oak Hill Cemetery

5. Artist Unknown, REST LAWN MAUSOLEUM RELIEFS

6. James A. Kuiper, SPLIT
   Mulick Park

7. Melville P. Steinfels and Harold Kerr, MOSES STRIKING THE ROCK
   Immaculate Heart of Mary Church

8. John R. Henry, UNTITLED
   Knollcrest Professional Building

9. Robert A. Jensen, JAUNT
   Calvin College

10. Artist Unknown, FATHER TIME
    Graceland Mausoleum

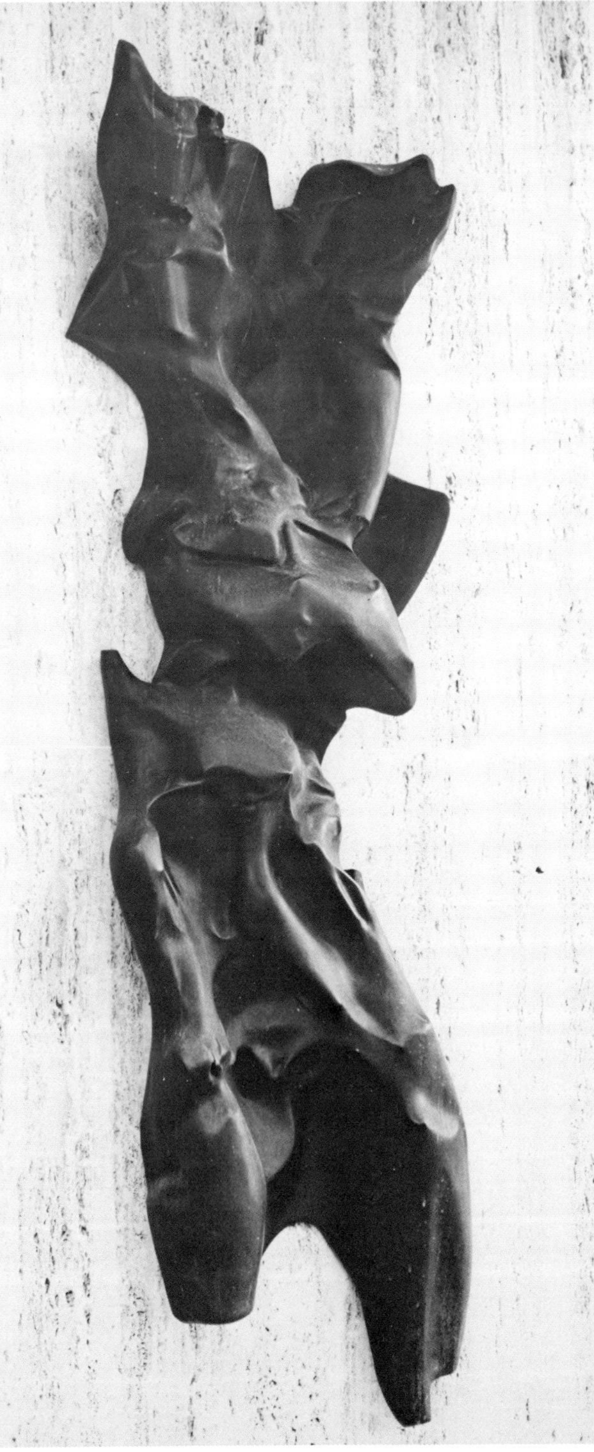

E-1

Calvin Albert (1918-)

BURNING BUSH

1973, bronze, 6'

Temple Emanuel
1715 E. Fulton, Grand Rapids

When this temple, designed by Erich Mendelsohn (1887-1953), was built, the congregation determined that works of art with aesthetic and inspirational value would be an integral part of the building. This expressively modeled *Burning Bush,* which graces the entry to the temple, was an especially interesting commission for Calvin Albert, a former temple member and Grand Rapids native. The bush which burns and is not consumed is associated with Moses and serves as an inspiration to the Jewish people who have suffered but endured.

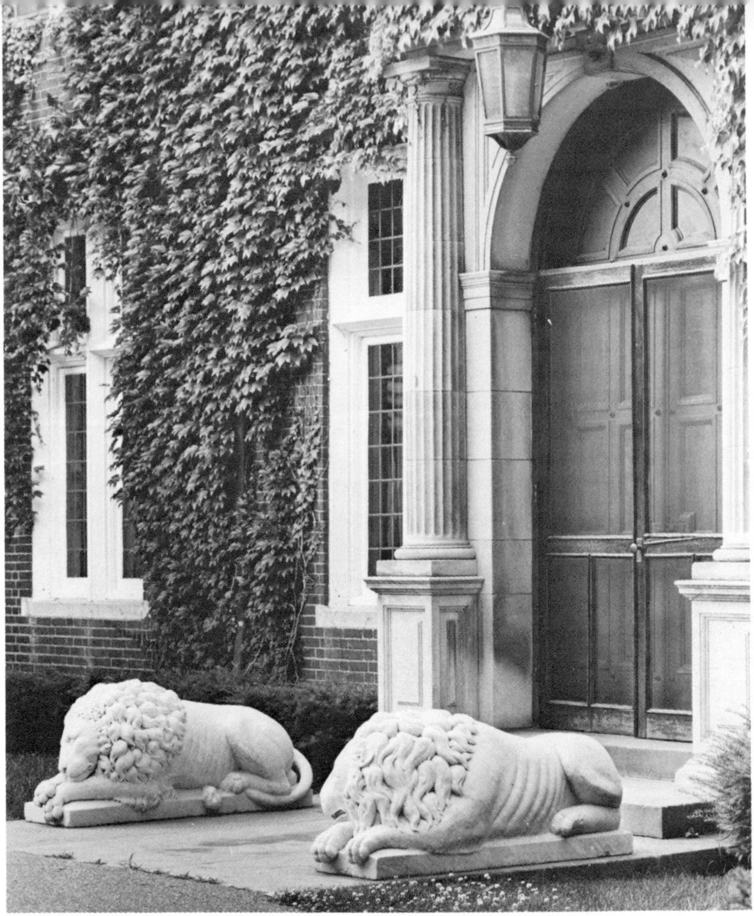

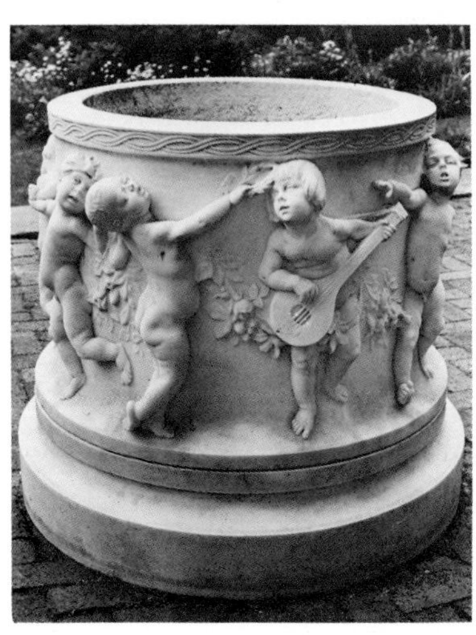

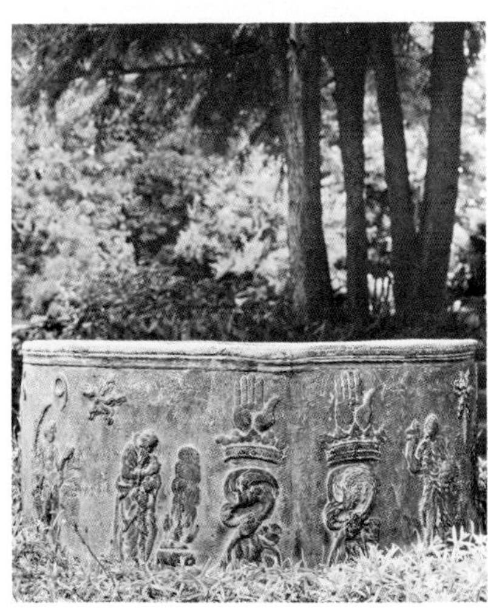

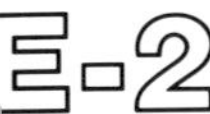

Artists Unknown

LIONS c. 1910, marble, 25″

URN c: 1910, marble, 35″

URN date unknown, lead, 13″

Sister's Residence, Saint Thomas Aquinas College (Holmdene)
E. Fulton, Grand Rapids

By 1906 plans were well under way for Holmdene, the estate of businessman Edward Lowe, Jr., and his wife, Susan R. Blodgett Lowe. The English character of the estate reflects the English ancestry of Lowe whose father came to Grand Rapids from Ashton-under-Lyne, England, in the 1860s. The Jacobethan Revival house was designed by Winslow and Bigelow of Boston. Landscape architects Ossian C. Simonds (1855-1931) of Chicago and Ellen B. Shipman (c. 1870-1950) of New York were responsible for the natural setting of the grounds and the formal terraced garden near the house. The lions which guard the entrance to the house were likely purchased on one of the family trips to Europe. Lions have been gateway guardians since antiquity, and the Lowes may have chosen lions because they are part of the Royal Arms of England. Urns have also been in use since antiquity, and these two are located in the terraced garden. The marble urn portrays singing and dancing children which are reminiscent of those carved by Renaissance sculptors Donatello (1386-1466) and Lucca della Robbia (1400-1482). One of the children on the urn is James Rowland Lowe who was born in 1904. It is not clear what is represented on the lead urn, but it, too, reflects classical influences.

Edward Lowe, Jr., died in 1938, and Holmdene was purchased in 1939 by the University of Grand Rapids (Davenport College). In 1945 the Dominican Sisters bought the property and Aquinas College moved from downtown Grand Rapids to a new campus.

Artist Unknown

A. B. WATSON MAUSOLEUM

1914, granite, *Sphinx* 38″

Oak Hill Cemetery
Hall and Eastern S.E., Grand Rapids

From around 1830-1850 and again in the early part of the twentieth century, there was an interest in Egyptian Revival architecture which is reflected in the construction of several mausoleums in Oak Hill Cemetery. In addition to the traditional tomb shape, Egyptian motifs include the sphinx, papyrus columns and capitals, and the winged sun disc on the cavetto or concave cornice. The mausoleum was constructed the year before the death of Martha A. Watson, Major Watson's wife, and his body was moved from the Valley City Cemetery vault to the mausoleum at the time of her funeral in 1915. Major Amasa Brown Watson (1826-1888), a Civil War veteran, made his fortune as a lumberman in Muskegon, Michigan. He moved to Grand Rapids around 1881 where he invested his money in several businesses, including the Fourth National Bank, the Grand Rapids Brush Company, and the A. B. Watson Veneer and Panel Company.

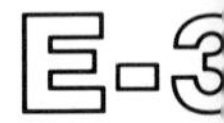

A. B. WATSON

Otto Vanselow

KENDALL MONUMENT

1900, limestone, 7′6″

[Designed by D. W. Kendall O. Vanselow Sculptor 1900]

Oak Hill Cemetery (Valley City Cemetery)
Hall and Eastern S.E., Grand Rapids

Shortly after her death, David W. Kendall (1851-1910) designed this unusual monument to place over the grave of his wife, Delle Colby Kendall (1852-1899). The surface of the large boulder is enlivened with Celtic interlace which enframes vignettes from the lives of the Kendalls. The boat commemorates a trip taken to the West Indies in 1897. Stormy seas during the trip are considered to have been the cause of Mrs. Kendall's death two years later. Below are David Kendall's illustrious ancestors, including John and Priscilla Alden, who provided eligibility for membership in the Massachusetts Society of Mayflower Descendants. Other memberships inscribed on the rock include Sons of the Revolution, Masonic Order, Benevolent and Protective Order of Elks, and the Ladies Literary Club. Grouped near the top are a dove, lion, and cross, symbols of the Christian faith. David Kendall came to Grand Rapids in 1879 as a designer for the Phoenix Furniture Company and played a role in the popularization of period furniture. The Kendall School of Design, in Grand Rapids, originally called the David Wolcott Kendall School of Art, was endowed in 1928 by Kendall's second wife, Helen M., as a memorial to her husband.

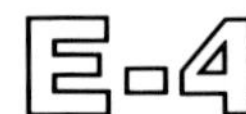

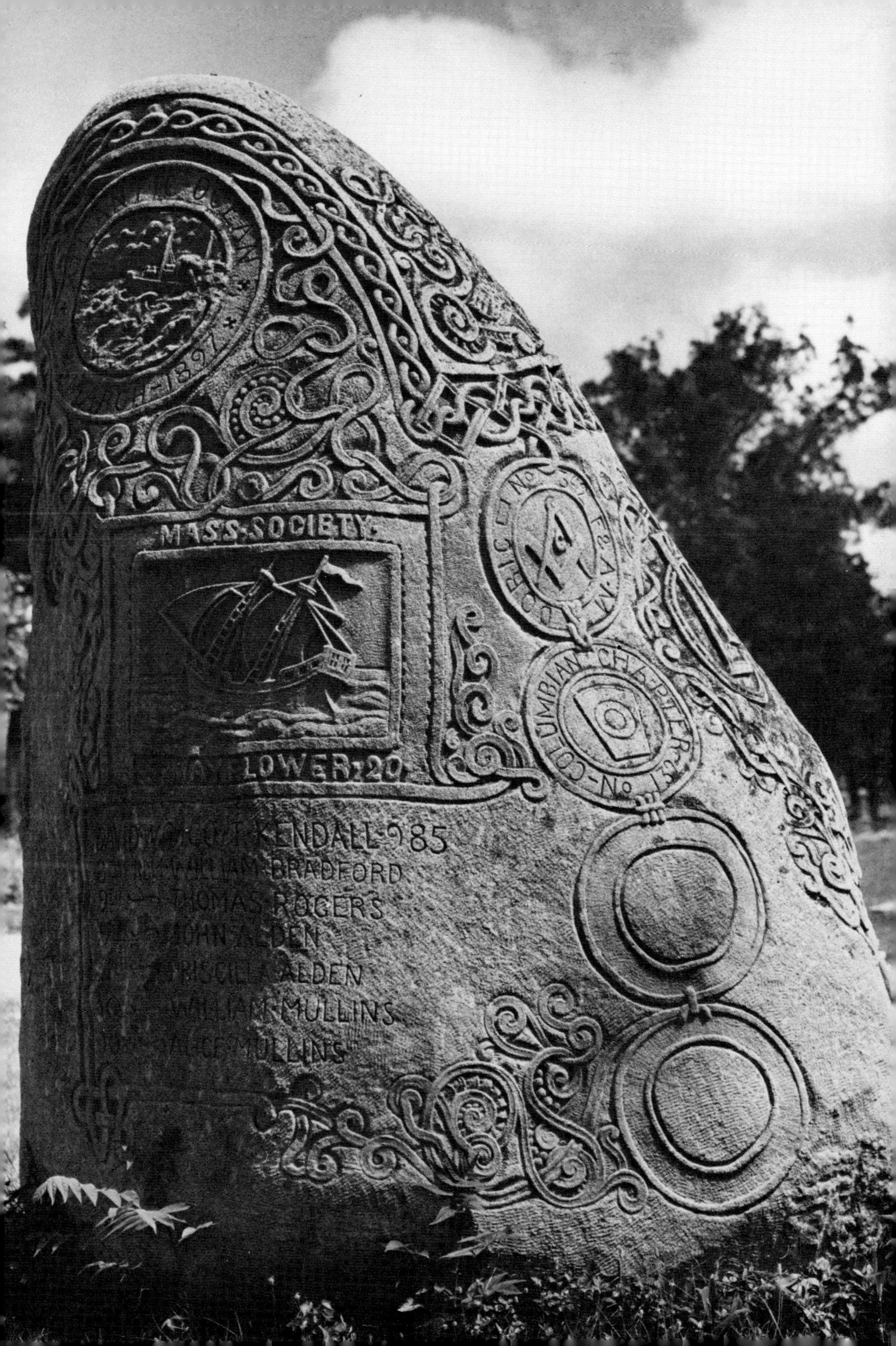
MASS SOCIETY
MAYFLOWER 20
KENDALL 985
WILLIAM BRADFORD
THOMAS ROGERS
JOHN ALDEN
PRISCILLA ALDEN
WILLIAM MULLINS
COLUMBIAN CHAPTER No 13

Artist Unknown

REST LAWN MAUSOLEUM RELIEFS

1932, limestone

Rest Lawn Mausoleum, Rest Lawn Memorial Park
3450 Eastern S.E., Grand Rapids

This Art Deco mausoleum was designed by Grand Rapids Architects Colton & Knecht to meet a growing interest in mausoleum burial. The firm had previously designed Graceland Mausoleum which opened around 1925. In addition to the herm-like figures which decorate the tower, swans are flanked by a sunrise. According to myth, the swan sings beautifully just before it dies, hence the expression swan song. The sculptural decoration of the building suggests that our farewell to this life is really the beginning of a new life after death. A plaque at the base of the building states that the tower of music was given in 1932 by Ruth Wernette in memory of her husband, D'Arcy L. Wernette, an engineer who died July 26, 1931.

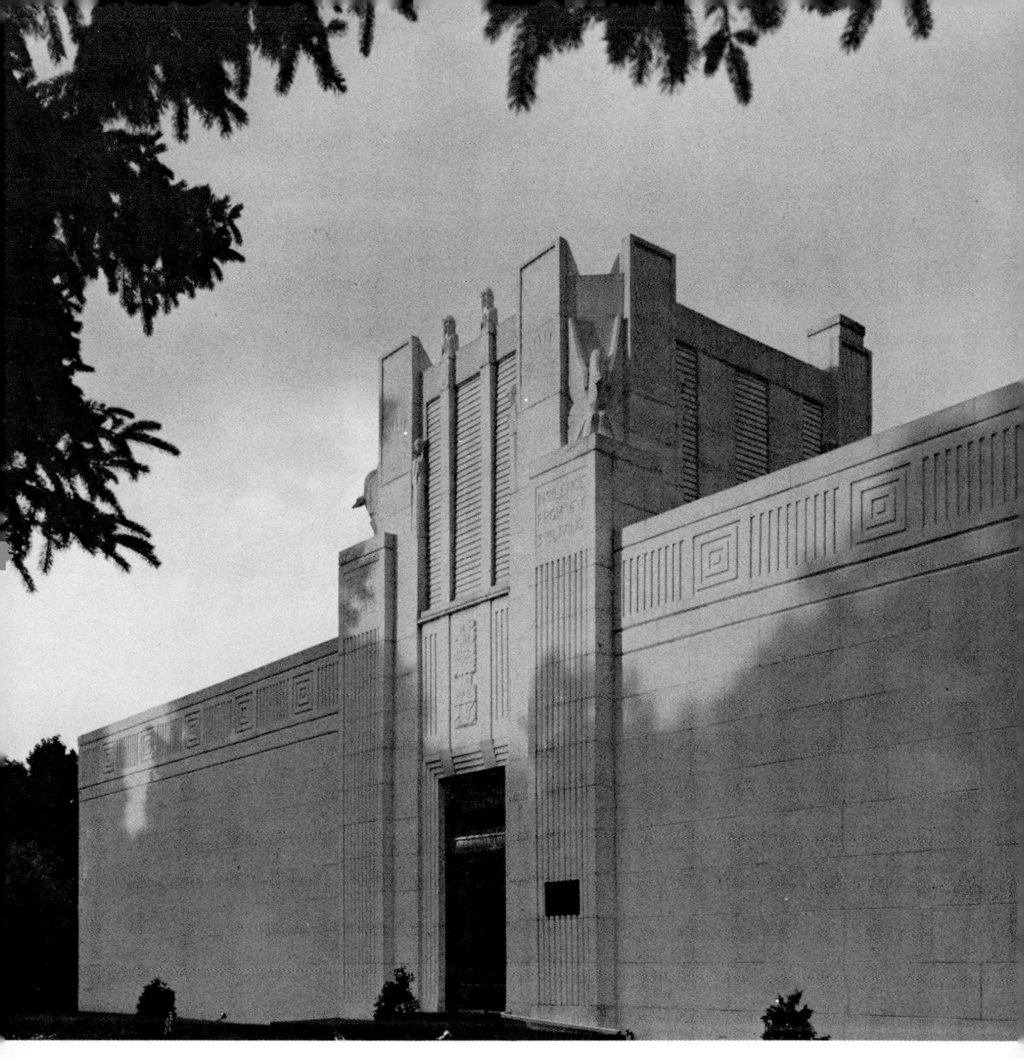

E-5

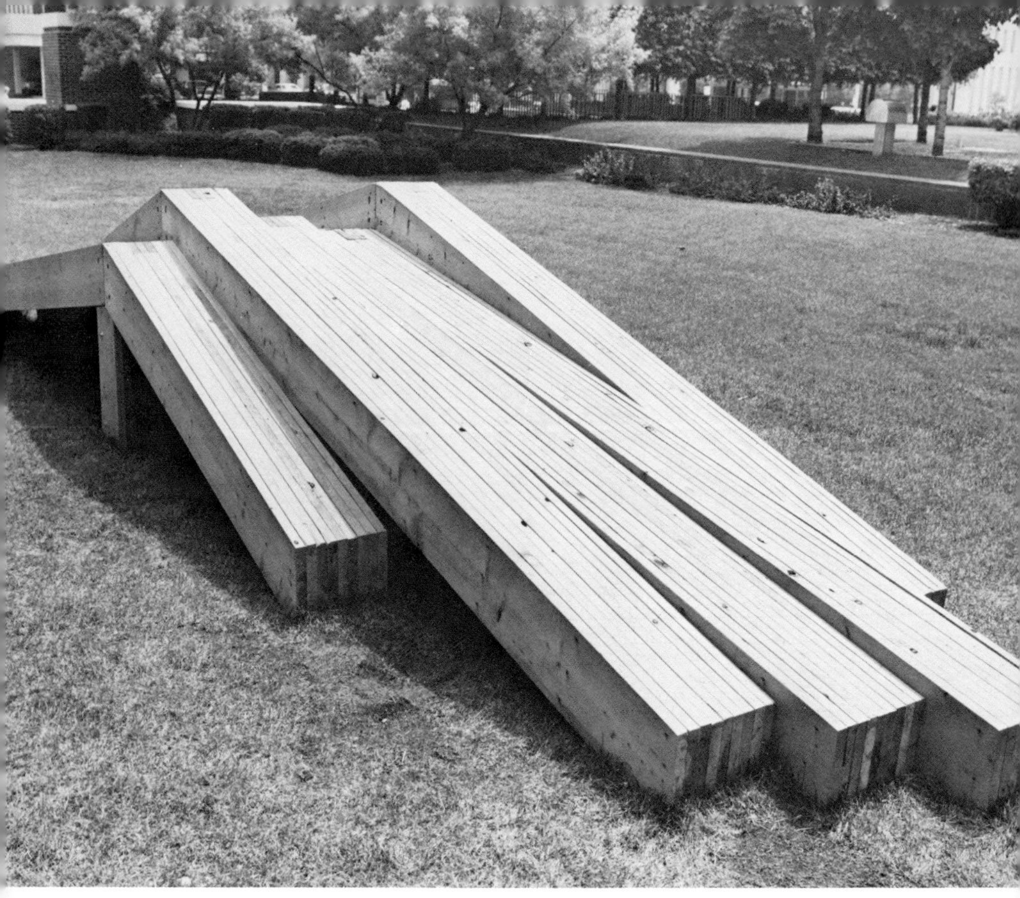

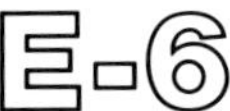

James A. Kuiper (1945-)

SPLIT

1979, wood, 4′6″

Mulick Park
Griggs and Sylvan S.E., Grand Rapids

The playground sculpture was commissioned for children to play on during Festival '79, Grand Rapids annual art celebration. It was later moved to its permanent location at Mulick Park where children continue to climb over and slide down its smooth surfaces. The linear piece is constructed of regular splits of wood which are laminated together to form five varying segments which are symmetrically repeated in each half or split of the work. The split is accentuated by the varying heights of the segments as they form angular junctures at the center of the work. Wood was chosen so that children might experience a soft material and as a reminder that Grand Rapids was once the Furniture City.

Melville P. Steinfels (1910-   ), Designer, and **Harold Kerr**

MOSES STRIKING THE ROCK

c. 1966, copper, 8′6″

Immaculate Heart of Mary Church
1935 Plymouth S.E., Grand Rapids

Immaculate Heart of Mary Church was designed by Detroit architect Charles D. Hannan (1909-   ) and dedicated on October 30, 1966. Outside the baptistry is the craggy statue of Moses designed by Melville P. Steinfels and executed by Harold Kerr. Moses is shown striking the rock with his rod to bring forth lifesaving water for the Israelites who wandered through the desert for forty years (Numbers 20:11). The figure of Moses originally stood in a pool of water which fed the baptismal font inside the baptistry. The pool represents the pool of Siloe, ancient source of water for Jerusalem. The water symbolizes the new life of the Christian as he enters the church through baptism.

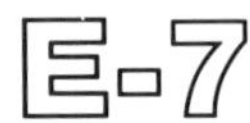

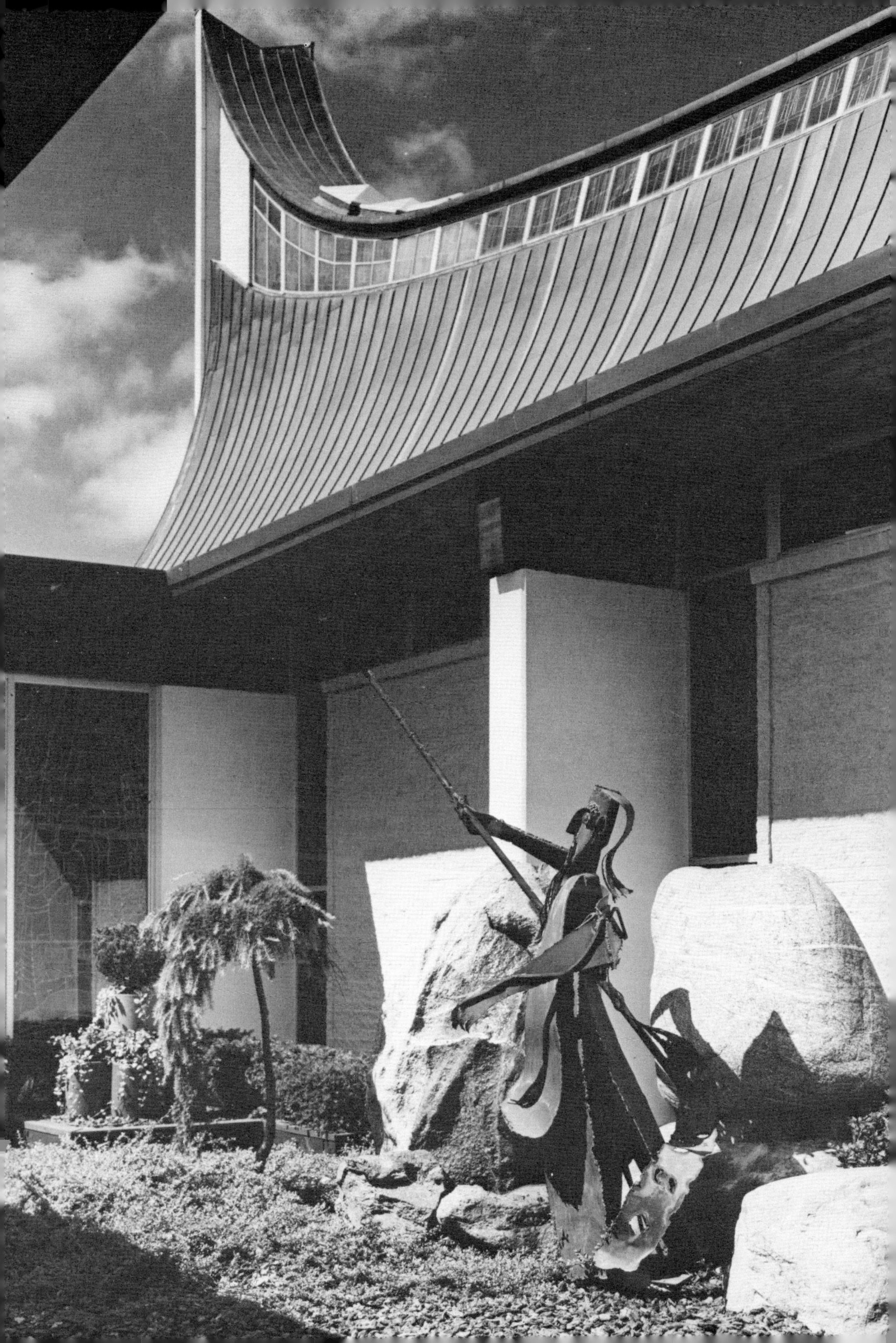

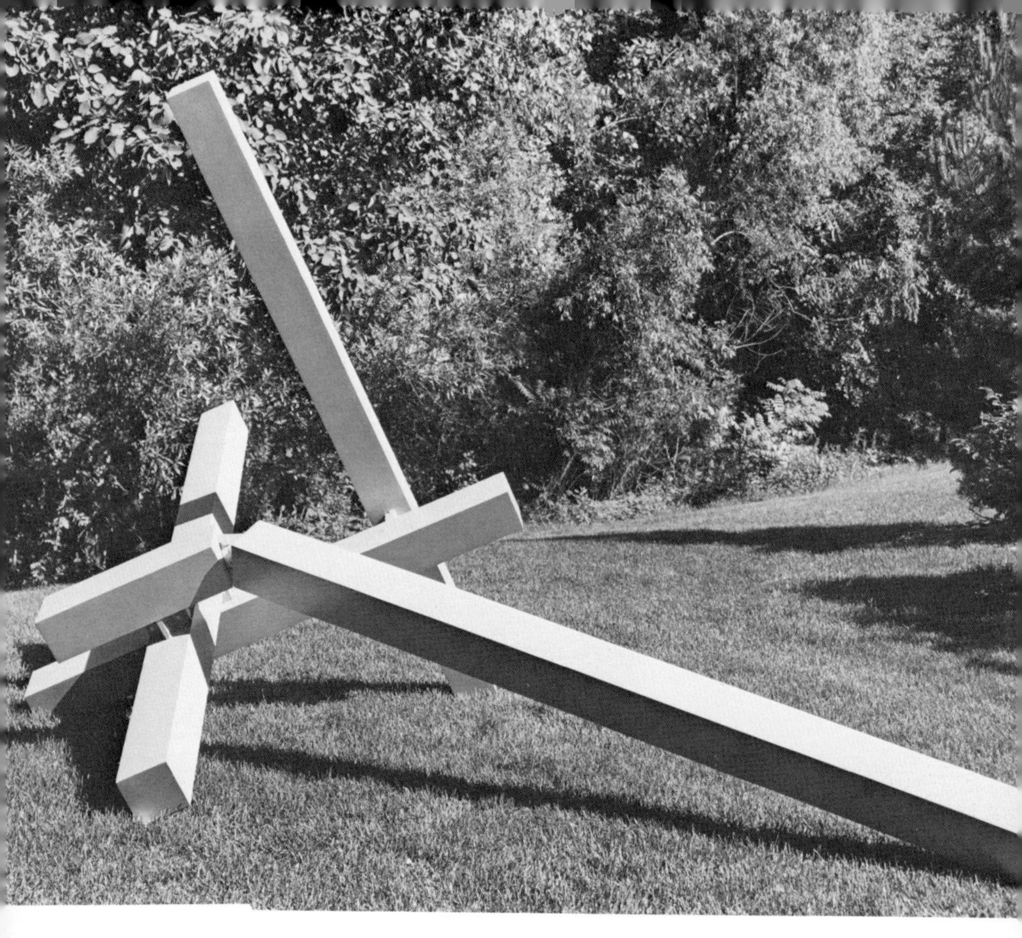

E-8

John R. Henry (1943-)

UNTITLED

1973, steel, 6′10″

Knollcrest Professional Building
3300 Burton S.E., Grand Rapids

In 1973, John Henry created *Landscape #4* for the Grand Rapids exhibition *Sculpture Off the Pedestal.* At the same time, he created this untitled work which was purchased for the new Knollcrest Professional Building through the efforts of Dr. James Oosting. Like all of Henry's works, this piece was personally constructed in his Chicago studio and reflects the industrial ambience of that city. The beams for this piece, formed from sheets of steel and joined by connectors, radiate, spiral, twist, and thrust out into space like yellow spokes.

Robert A. (Robin) Jensen (1930-)

JAUNT

1977, epoxy resin and fiber glass over polystyrene core, 7′8″

[Robert Jensen]

College Center, Calvin College
E. Beltline, Grand Rapids

Jaunt was created as part of a *Jauntin'* series during Robin Jensen's sabbatical at Calvin College in 1977. This particular work was placed near the College Center Building so that children attending classes in the Education Department could respond to and test the sculpture. Inspired by the biblical story of Jonah and the whale, this sculpture suggests the fluid motion of fish and water and Jonah's joy when he was delivered from the whale. The various planes of this biomorphic form are heightened by orange, yellow, and blue paint and add to the joyous feeling. The viewer is invited to take a juant over, through, and around the sculpture. For Jensen, the *Jauntin'* series reflects a life journey full of creative adventures which glorify God.

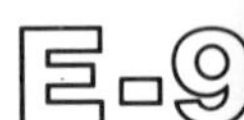

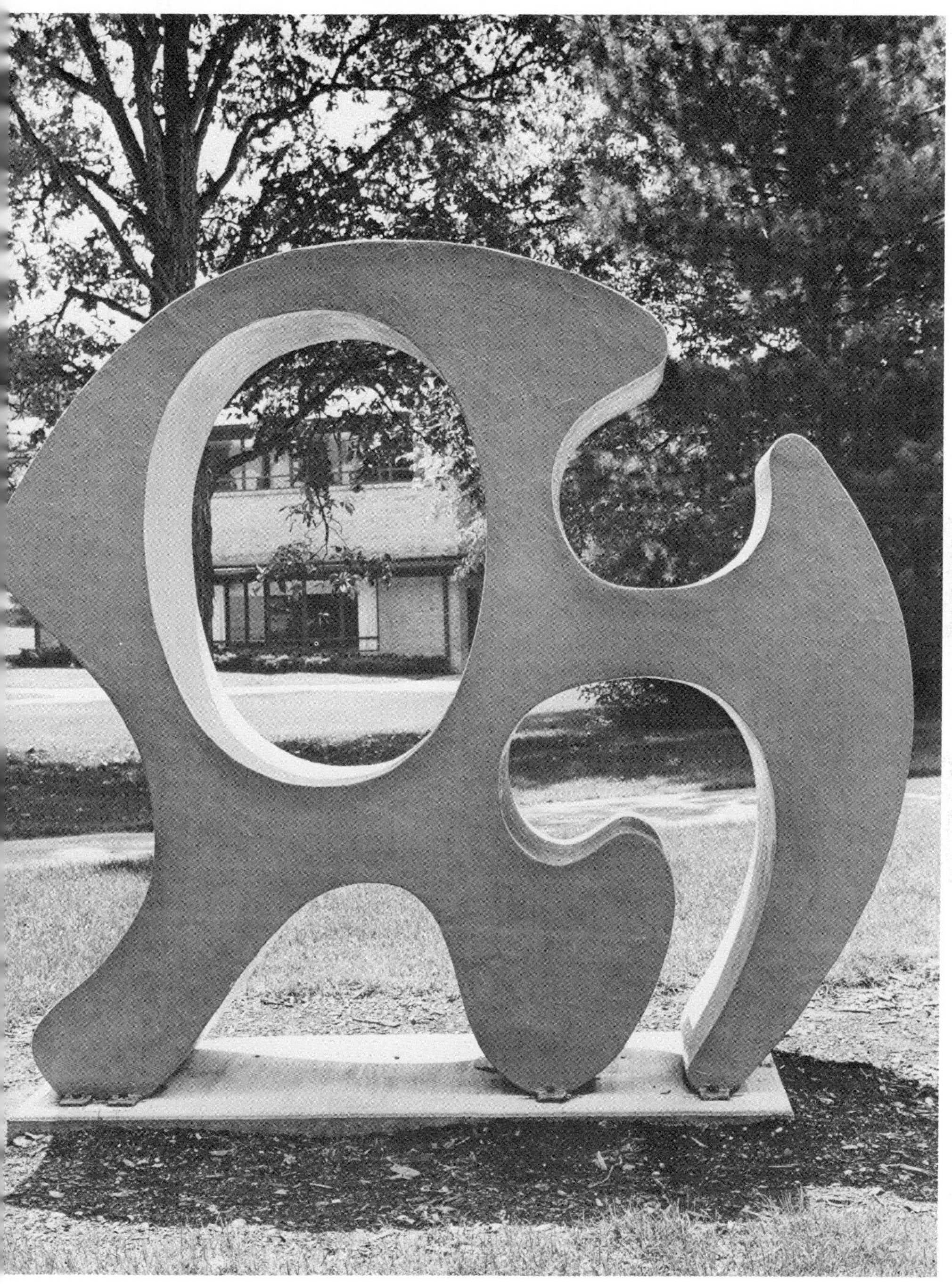

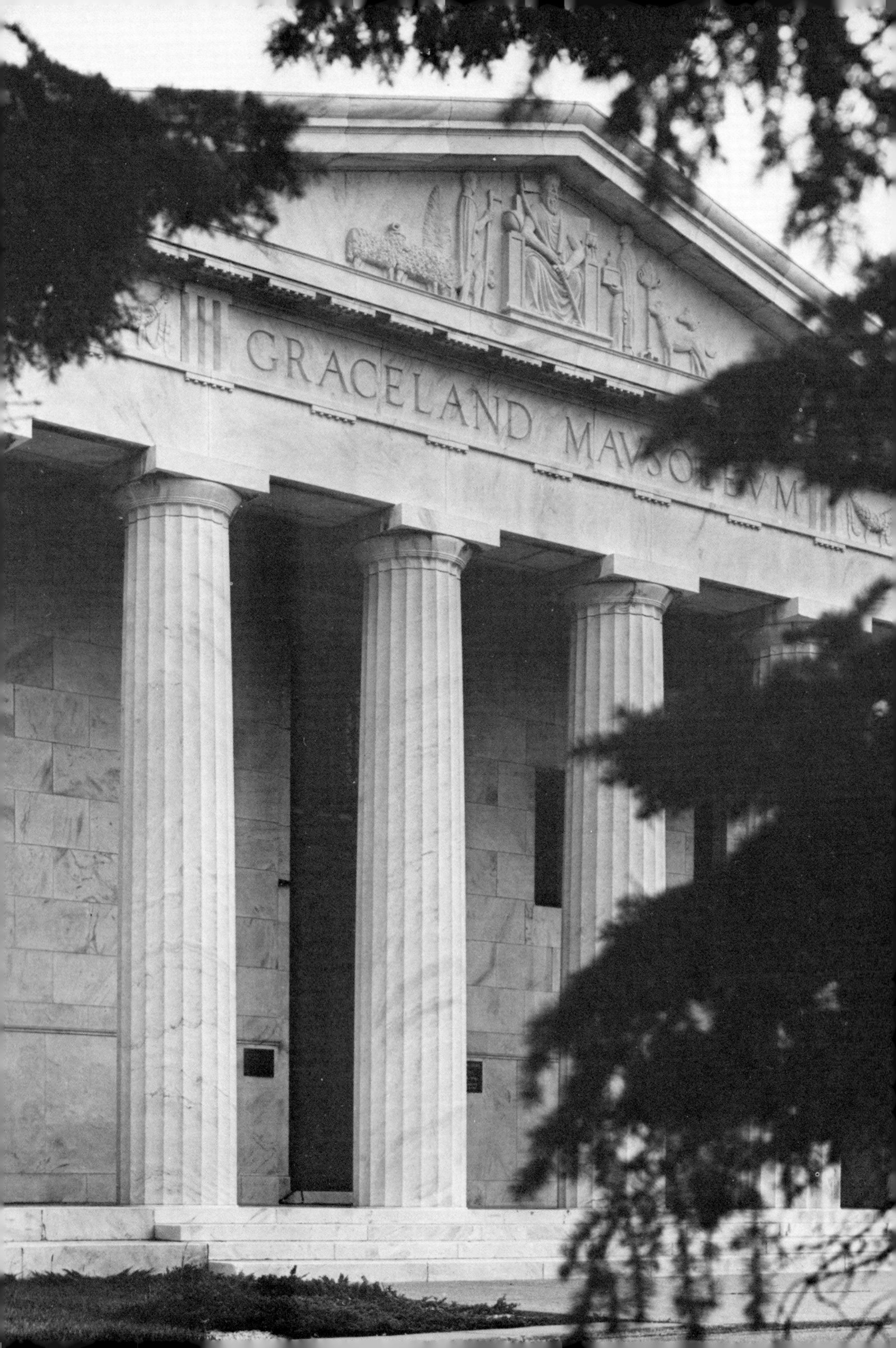
GRACELAND MAVSOLEVM

E-10

Artist Unknown

FATHER TIME

c. 1924, marble, c. 6′

Graceland Mausoleum
4341 Cascade Road S.E., Grand Rapids

Though mausoleum burial has been known since antiquity, it was promoted around the turn of the century as a progressive burial method. This mausoleum, which was designed by Grand Rapids architects Colton and Knecht, is based on the design of a Greek Doric temple. The Georgia Marble Company of Atlanta, Georgia, provided the marble and the carving for the building. The scene contained within the pediment portrays Father Time approached by a shepherd and a man bearing a chest with a crown on top of it. This scene suggests that rich or poor, all must bow to Father Time.

ARTISTS' BIOGRAPHIES

CALVIN ALBERT (1918-)
A native of Grand Rapids, Albert studied at the Grand Rapids Art Gallery with Otto Karl Bach, the Chicago Art Institute, the Chicago Institute of Design with László Moholy-Nagy and György Kepes, and at the Archipenko School of Sculpture. He received a Fullbright grant in 1961, Tiffany grants in 1963 and 1965, and a Guggenheim Fellowship in 1966. He taught at the Chicago Institute of Design from 1942 to 1946, Brooklyn College from 1947 to 1949, and has taught at the Pratt Institute since 1949. His works include Ark Doors and Candelabra, Steinberg House, Park Avenue Synagogue, New York, 1954; Outdoor Candelabra, Temple Israel, Tulsa, 1955; Eternal Light and Candelabra, Temple Israel, Bridgeport, Connecticut, 1957; Crucifix, Tabernacle, and Candlesticks, St. Paul's, Peoria, Illinois, 1959; and *Burning Bush,* Temple Emanuel, Grand Rapids, Michigan, 1973.

ALEXANDER CALDER (1898-1976)
Born in Philadelphia, the son and grandson of noted sculptors, Calder received a degree in mechanical engineering from Stevens Institute of Technology, Hoboken, New Jersey, in 1919. He studied at the Art Students League with John Sloan and others from 1923 to 1926. He settled in Paris and began to create a miniature circus exploring drawing with wire and motion. By the 1930s Calder began to use abstract forms to create stabiles, stationary works which suggest motion, and mobiles, sculptures with moving parts. Among his numerous works are *The Spiral,* Paris, 1948; *Teodelapio,* Spoleto, Italy, 1962; *Four Elements,* Stockholm, 1962; *Hello Girls!,* Los Angeles County Art Museum, 1964; *Ghost,* Guggenheim Museum, New York, 1964; and *La Grande Vitesse,* Grand Rapids, Michigan, 1969.

HORACE F. COLBY (1901-1966)
Born in Harbor Point, Michigan, Colby lived in Detroit until he moved to Pasadena, California, in the early 1930s. He received a B.F.A. from Cornell University in 1924. After graduation he studied at the American Academy in Rome and served as a sculptor for the University of Michigan's Expedition to Pisidian Antioch. His works include *Zoltan Sepeshy,* Cranbrook Museum, Bloomfield Hills, Michigan, 1928 and *Captain Charles E. Belknap,* Belknap Memorial Park, Grand Rapids, Michigan, 1931.

POMPEO L. COPPINI (1870-1957)
Born in Moglia, Italy, Coppini graduated from the Academy of Fine Arts in Florence in 1889. He came to New York in 1896 and later had studios in Chicago and San Antonio. In the latter city he was head of the Fine Arts Department at Trinity University from 1943 to 1945 and founded the Coppini Academy of Fine Arts. His many commissions include *Richard B. Westnedge,* Kalamazoo, Michigan, 1900; *George Washington,* Mexico City, 1911; *James P. Clarke,* Statuary Hall, Washington, D.C., 1918; *General William Rufus Shafter,* Galesburg, Michigan, 1919; *John Ball Memorial,* Grand Rapids, Michigan, 1925; and the *Spirit of Sacrifice,* Alamo Heroes Cenotaph, San Antonio, Texas, 1936.

LEON COQUARD (1860-1923)
Born in Detroit, Coquard was educated in the parochial schools. By 1882, he was employed as a draughtsman for the Detroit architect Albert E. French. Coquard opened his own architectural firm around 1887 and specialized in churches. He is known for his design of Sainte Anne's Church, Detroit, Michigan, 1887. He may also have designed the *Soldiers' Monument* which was unveiled in Grand Rapids, Michigan, on September 17, 1885. Coquard's name appeared on a drawing which was featured in the Grand Rapids *Daily Democrat* (September 11, 1885:1) and the *Grand Rapids Daily Eagle* (September 17, 1885:10).

WILLIAM COUPER (1853-1942)
Born in Norfolk, Virginia, Couper became familiar with sculpture in his father's firm, Couper Marble Works, which was located in Richmond, Virginia. After study at Cooper Institute in New York, he entered the Academy of Fine Arts and the Royal College of Surgery in Munich. In 1875 he went to Florence where he shared a studio with Thomas Ball (1819-1911) and married Ball's daughter in 1878. He and Ball returned to New York in 1897 where they continued to share a studio. Among Couper's many works are his *Moses* for the Appellate Court, New York; *President William McKinley,* Albright Library, Scranton, Pennsylvania; *Beauty's Wreath for Valor's Brow; Sailors of the Revolution,* Memorial Hall, Annapolis, Maryland; and *Henry Wadsworth Longfellow,* Grand Rapids, Michigan. He also completed a seated statue of Longfellow in 1909 which was begun by Ball and is located in Washington, D.C.

ROBBIN L. CRAWFORD (1937-)
A Grand Rapids native, Crawford graduated from Ottawa Hills High School in 1955. While there he received a tool and die background and has been employed as a machine designer. The Grand Rapids works of this self-taught sculptor include *Cantilivered Chime,* City Hall, 1974; *Yellow Participating Triangula,* Dickinson School, 1975; *GI's Revenge,* County Building, 1976; and *Orange-Ganic Domino,* John Ball Memorial Park, 1977.

RALPH W. DEMMON (1894-1978)
Born in Grand Rapids, Demmon graduated from Central High School. He attended Michigan Agricultural College and received a B.A. in architecture from the University of Michigan in 1923. After graduation he was employed in the State Architect's Office in Ann Arbor until he returned to Grand Rapids. From 1924 to 1927 he worked for the firm of Osgood and Osgood and opened his own architectural firm in 1927. Demmon, who specialized in residential architecture, designed the *Memorial Pillars,* Veterans Memorial Park, Grand Rapids, 1926. He also designed, among other things, furniture and jewelry.

MARK DI SUVERO (1933-)
Born in Shanghai of Italian parents, di Suvero came to California with his family in 1941. He attended San Francisco City College from 1953 to 1954 and transferred first to the University of California at Santa Barbara and then to the University of California at Berkeley. He received a B.A. in philosophy from the latter institution in 1957 and left for New York. He was one of the first sculptors in the 1960s to begin creating large outdoor works, often incorporating rough wood and found objects. He chose to live in Europe from 1971 to 1975 as a protest against the Vietnam War. His works include *Tom,* Detroit Institute of Arts, 1959; *Praise for Elohim Adonai,* St. Louis Art Museum, 1966; *For Lady Day,* Park Forest South, Illinois, 1968-1969; *K Piece,* Kröller-Müller Museum, Otterloo, Netherlands, 1971-1972; *Étoile Polaire,* Grenoble, France, 1973; and *Motu,* Grand Rapids, Michigan, 1977.

ATTILIO D. GANDOLA (1884-1930)
PAOLA M. GANDOLA (1889-1963)
Born in northern Italy, the brothers founded the Gandola Brothers Monument and Architectural Works in Cleveland, Ohio. While in Italy, Attilio spent four years studying drawing and carving. He worked in France six months before immigrating to the United States shortly after the turn of the century. Before settling permanently in Cleveland, Attilio executed carvings around the country. After Paola (Paul) graduated from the Royal Academy of Fine Arts and the Castel Sforzesco in Milan, he joined his brother in Cleveland. The firm executed carvings for many buildings including the Angels with Golden Trumpets, St. Adalbert, Grand Rapids, Michigan, c. 1910; Utah State Capitol, Mormon Church, Salt Lake City, Utah; City Hall, City Hospital, Wagner Monument, Cleveland, Ohio; and *Cain* and *Abel,* Lake County Courthouse, Painesville, Ohio.

JASHA GREEN (1927-)
Born in Boston, Massachusetts, Green studied at the Boston Museum School and with Fernand Léger (1881-1955) in Paris. He gained welding experience while working in a Boston steel mill. Both a painter and a sculptor, his works can be found at the Solomon R. Guggenheim Museum, the Brooklyn Museum, the Israel Museum, the Phoenix Art Museum, and the Santa Barbara Museum of Art. *Floor Kite XIV* of 1977 is located at the Grand Rapids Art Museum, Grand Rapids, Michigan.

JOHN R. HENRY (1943-)
Born in Lexington, Kentucky, Henry attended the University of Kentucky, the University of Washington, the School of the Chicago Art Institute, the University of Chicago, and the Illinois Institute of Technology, Chicago. He has been a Visiting Professor at the following schools: the University of Iowa, 1969; the University of Wisconsin, 1970; the University of Chicago, 1971; and Aquinas College, Grand Rapids, Michigan, 1974. His works include an untitled sculpture for the Knollcrest Professional Building, Grand Rapids, Michigan, 1973; *Sun Target I,* Mint Museum of Art, Charlotte, North Carolina, 1974; *Illinois Landscape #5,* Governors State University, Park Forest South, Illinois, 1976; and *Sioux City,* Sioux City, Iowa, 1978.

NATHAN HOROWITZ (1947-)
Born in Grand Rapids, Horowitz attended Grand Valley State College and received a B.F.A. from Aquinas College in 1971 and an M.F.A. from Cranbrook Academy of Art in 1973. His works include a Menorah, Temple Emanuel, Grand Rapids, 1970; *Purity* and *Chastity,* Michigan Life/National Casualty Building (across from Tel-12 Mall), Southfield, Michigan, 1973; *Vesta,* County Building, Grand Rapids, 1973; and *Honey, What Did You Say Your First Name Was?* Bloomfield Hills School District, Bloomfield Hills, 1974.

ROBERT A. (ROBIN) JENSEN (1930-)
Born in Elyria, Ohio, Jensen received a B.F.A. in 1951 and an M.F.A. in 1952 from Ohio University. He also did advanced graduate work at Miami University, Ohio, in 1961. From 1952 to 1961 he served as an artist, illustrator, and Visual Information Specialist for the federal government. He taught at Madison High School, West Middletown, Ohio, from 1962 to 1964 and has taught at Calvin College since 1964. His works in Grand Rapids include *Pentecost,* Shawnee Park Christian Reformed Church, 1968; *Jaunt,* Calvin College, 1977; and *Earth Loops,* John Ball Memorial Park, 1978.

HAROLD KERR
Kerr executed Melville P. Steinfels' design for *Moses Striking the Rock,* Immaculate Heart of Mary Church, Grand Rapids, Michigan, c. 1966.

JOSEPH E. KINNEBREW IV (1942-)
Born in Tacoma, Washington, Kinnebrew received a B.A. from Syracuse University in 1964 and an M.F.A. from Michigan State Univeristy in 1970. Among Kinnebrew's works are an untitled sculpture, Harris Bank & Trust, Chicago, 1967; *Diagrams,* University of San Francisco, 1974; untitled work, Wayne State Health Care Institute, Detroit, 1979; and the *William A. Brenke River Sculpture/Fish Ladder,* Lansing, Michigan, scheduled to be completed in 1980. His Grand Rapids, Michigan, works include *Stroll,* Grand Rapids Junior College, c. 1973; *Grand River Sculpture and Fish Ladder,* 1974; *Kid Katwalk,* Sixth Street Bridge Park, 1975; and *Here Man's Desire*...("Justice"), Hall of Justice, 1978.

THEODORE ALICE RUGGLES KITSON (1871-1932)
Born in Brookline, Massachusetts, Kitson studied in Paris with Dagan-Bouveret. She received honorable mention at both the Paris Exposition in 1889 and the Paris Salon of 1890, the latter award being the first ever given to an American woman. She also

studied with the American sculptor Henry Hudson Kitson (1865-1947) whom she married in 1893. She executed many public sculptures which are located throughout the United States, including *Kosciusko,* Boston, Massachusetts; *Victory,* Hingham, Massachusetts; the *Volunteer of '61,* Newburyport, Massachusetts, 1902; eight portrait medallions for the General Sherman Monument, Washington, D.C., 1903; and *The Hiker,* Minneapolis, Minnesota. Approximately fifty castings have been made of the latter, including three in Michigan, in the cities of Grand Rapids, c. 1927, Kalamazoo, c. 1923, and Lansing, c. 1945. The last *Hiker* was erected in Washington, D.C. in 1964.

JAMES A. KUIPER (1945-   )
Born in Roseland, Illinois, Kuiper attended Trinity Christian College, Palos Heights, Illinois, from 1964 to 1965; Calvin College, Grand Rapids, Michigan, from 1965 to 1968; and Michigan State University from 1974 to 1976. He received a B.A. from Calvin College in 1968 and an M.F.A. from Michigan State University in 1976. After teaching English in Gboko, Nigeria, West Africa, from 1968 to 1971, Kuiper was an art therapist at Pine Rest Christian Hospital, Cutlerville, Michigan from 1971 to 1973. He also taught at Grand Rapids Christian High School from 1973 to 1977 and has been teaching at Calvin College since 1977. His works include *Jazz Here,* Flint Institute of Art, Flint, Michigan, 1975; *Abraxos,* Grand Rapids Art Museum, Grand Rapids, Michigan, 1976-1979; *Abraxos VII,* Coopers and Lybrand Associates, Grand Rapids, Michigan, 1979; *Salomé*, Steelcase Incorporated, St. Louis, Missouri, 1979; and *Split,* Mulick Park, Grand Rapids, Michigan, 1979.

THOMAS LEECH (c. 1951-   )
Leech received a B.F.A. from Aquinas College and later attended Virginia Commonwealth University in Richmond, Virginia. His works in Grand Rapids include *Sizby,* Grand Rapids Public Library, 1973, and several play sculptures which were created for Festival '73 and are now in John Ball Memorial Park.

ROBERT MORRIS (1931-)
Born in Kansas City, Morris studied at the following schools from 1948 to 1955: Kansas City Art Institute, University of Kansas City, California School of Fine Arts, and Reed College. He received an M.A. from Hunter College in 1966 and has taught at that school since 1967. Morris received a Guggenheim Fellowship in 1969. His numerous works include *Steam Piece,* West Washington University, Bellingham, Washington, 1969; *Observatory,* Sonsbeek, the Netherlands, 1971; *Labyrinth,* Institute of Contemporary Art, Philadelphia, 1974; and *Grand Rapids Project ("X")* Grand Rapids, Michigan, 1974.

CORRADO JOSEPH PARDUCCI (1900-)
Born in Pisa, Italy, Parducci came to New York in 1904 and graduated from P.S. 95 in 1915. He was introduced to architectural modeling when he began working for Donnelly and Ricci and served an apprenticeship with Ricci and Zari from 1917 to 1921. While in New York he studied at the Beaux-Arts Institute of Design and with George Bridgman at the Art Students League. After the apprenticeship, he was employed by Anthony di Lorenzo who sent him to Detroit in 1924. Parducci stayed on and opened his own studio in 1925. His numerous commissions can be found throughout the United States. Among his Detroit works are the Bear Fountain at the Zoo, the Buhl, Fisher, and Guardian buildings, Meadowbrook Hall, and the Music Hall Theater. His Lansing works include the First Baptist Church, Pilgrim Congregational Church, Grace Lutheran Church, St. Paul's Episcopal Church, Lansing Bell Telephone Company, and Sexton High School. His works can also be found on the Kalamazoo County Building, Kalamazoo, Michigan, and the Grand Rapids Civic Auditorium and the Michigan National Bank Building (Grand Rapids Trust), Grand Rapids, Michigan.

MARY GARDNER PREMINGER (c. 1926-)
A native of Grand Rapids, Preminger received a design scholarship to the Kansas City Art Museum when she was sixteen years old. She has also studied at the École des Beaux-Arts in Paris and with Fritz Faiss at the University of California, Los Angeles, 1954-1956. Besides Preminger's *Recreform,* John Ball Memorial Park, Grand Rapids, 1974, her works can be found at Briarwood Mall, Ann Arbor, Michigan; Inland Steel Corporation, Chicago; Security Pacific Bank, Los Angeles; and Golden Gate Park, San Francisco.

MELVILLE P. STEINFELS (1910-)
Born in Salt Lake City, Utah, Steinfels studied at the Chicago Art Institute from 1928 to 1932 and was artist-in-residence at Sienna Heights College, Adrian, Michigan, from 1945 to 1950. A painter and designer, his many works include a mosaic of the Glorified Cross and the sculpture design for *Moses Striking the Rock,* Immaculate Heart of Mary Church, Grand Rapids, 1966; frescoes, Our Lady of Lourdes Church, Indianapolis; ceramic tile murals, University of Detroit High School; and mosaics of the Psalms, Gallery of the Psalms, All Saints Mausoleum, Des Plaines, Illinois, 1977.

LORETTA STEPHENSON (1938-)
Born in Edmonton, Alberta, Canada, Stephenson graduated from Royal Oak High School in 1956. She served as an apprentice to Grand Rapids printmaker Marjorie Kloster from 1961 to 1968 and also studied with Hal Jones at Kalamazoo College in 1966. Among her works which are not in private collections are the untitled sculpture, Sears Mini-Park, Grand Rapids, Michigan, 1972, and *Tree Form,* Mr. Burt, Ada, Michigan, 1973.

LORADO TAFT (1860-1936)
Born in Elmwood, Illinois, Taft received a B.A. in 1879 and an M.A. in 1880 from the University of Illinois. He studied in Paris at the École des Beaux-Arts from 1880 to 1883 and independently from 1884 to 1886. He taught at the Chicago Art Institute from 1886 to 1929 and began teaching at the University of Chicago in 1892 and the University of Illinois in 1919. Taft also lectured and wrote extensively on sculpture and made a major contribution to the history of art with his book the *History of American Sculpture* (1903). Taft's numerous works include *The Sleep of the Flowers* and *The Awakening of the Flowers,* Horticulture Building, World's Columbian Exposition, 1893; *Thomas D. Gilbert,* Veterans Memorial Park, Grand Rapids, Michigan, 1895; *Defense of the Flag,* Jackson, Michigan, 1903; *Black Hawk,* Oregon, Illinois, 1911; *Columbus Fountain,* Washington, D.C., 1912; *Fountain of the Great Lakes,* Grant Park, Chicago, 1913; *Memory,* Woodland Cemetery, Jackson, Michigan, 1923; and *Charles Henry Hackley,* Muskegon, Michigan, 1929.

BARBARA (BOBBIE) C. UHL (1925-)
Born in Grand Rapids, Uhl received a B.A. from Bennington College in 1947 and since 1959 has enrolled in several art courses. From 1974 to 1976 she was Artist in the Schools for the Grand Rapids public school system. Her works include an untitled painting, City Hall, Grand Rapids, 1971; *Choir Director,* Fountain Street Church, Grand Rapids, 1974; untitled sculpture, Fountain Street Church, Grand Rapids, 1975; and an untitled silk screen painting, Board of Education Building, Grand Rapids, 1976.

OTTO VANSELOW
Vanselow was a German sculptor and model maker who is known to have been in Grand Rapids from 1892 to 1900. From 1892 to 1897 he was a partner with Adolph C. Bodelak, a woodcarver and designer, in the firm of Bodelak & Vanselow. He carved the Kendall Monument, Oakhill Cemetery, Grand Rapids, Michigan, in 1900.

B. WATHOF AND SON
The rooster weathervane located on the Central Reformed Church, Grand Rapids, Michigan, was created by the firm of B. Wathof and Son in 1957. The firm, located in Goor in the Netherlands, has made weathervanes for churches for several generations.

RONALD WATSON (1941-)
Born in Grand Island, Nebraska, Watson received a B.F.A. in 1964 and an M.F.A. in 1967 from the University of Nebraska. He taught at Northern Michigan University from 1967 to 1968 and has taught at Aquinas College from 1968 to the present where he has also been Chairperson of the Art Department since 1971. His works include an untitled sculpture, Ferris State College, Big Rapids, Michigan, c. 1974; *Molly's Cloud,* Grand Rapids Art Museum, Grand Rapids, Michigan, 1972; *Solar Painting: The Terminator,* Justice Park, Grand Rapids, Michigan, 1975; *Chopin Color Study,* Coopers and Lybrand, Inc., Grand Rapids, Michigan, 1976; untitled sculpture, Robert Vogel Interprises, Inc., Chicago, c. 1977.

ADOLPH A. WEINMAN (1870-1952)
Born in Karlsruhe, Germany, Weinman came to New York in 1880 where he was apprenticed to Frederick Kaldenberg, a wood and ivory carver. During his apprenticeship, he attended classes at Cooper Union. He later studied at the Art Students League with Augustus Saint-Gaudens (1848-1907) and in 1890 he entered the studio of Philip Martiny (1858-1927). Before opening his own studio in 1905, he worked with well-known American sculptors Olin Warner (1844-1896), Augustus Saint-Gaudens, Charles Niehaus (1885-1935), and Daniel Chester French (1850-1931). His numerous works include *The Destiny of the Redman,* St. Louis Exposition, 1904; *General Alexander Macomb,* Detroit, Michigan, 1906-1908; *Abraham Lincoln,* Lincoln Place, Grand Rapids, Michigan, c. 1913; the United States Mercury dime and half dollar,

(Continued on next page)

1916; *Descending Night, Rising Day,* Krannert Art Museum, University of Illinois, Urbana-Champaign, n.d.; Department of the Post Office Building, Washington, D.C., 1934; and *Oscar S. Strauss Memorial Fountain,* Washington, D.C., 1947.

LUMEN MARTIN WINTER (1908-)
Born in Ellery, Illinois, Winter came to Grand Rapids as a small child. He graduated from Grand Rapids Junior College in 1928 and from the Cleveland School of Art in 1929. He also studied in New York at the National Academy of Design, the Beaux-Arts Institute of Design, and the Grant Central Schools of Art. Winter is a painter, sculptor, and designer, and his many works include the *Conversion of St. Paul,* Church of St. Paul the Apostle, New York; the Apollo 13 Flight Medallion, 1970; *Labor Is Life,* AFL-CIO Headquarters Building, Washington, D.C., 1972; *Titans,* United Nations Building, New York, 1972; and *The Legend of Grand Rapids,* Gerald R. Ford Health and Education Center, Grand Rapids, 1976.

HY ZELKOWITZ (1946-)
Born in Brooklyn, New York, Zelkowitz attended Brooklyn College from 1963 to 1966 and Syracuse University from 1966 to 1970 where he received a B.I.D. He was an artist-in-residence through the Michigan Council for the Arts Artist-in-Residence Program at Pierce Elementary School, Flint, Michigan, in 1977. He is currently employed as a designer for Knoll International, East Greenville, Pennsylvania. His Grand Rapids works include *Lorrie's Button,* West Riverbank Park, 1976, and *On Having the Last Word,* Grand Rapids Art Museum, 1978.

SELECT BIBLIOGRAPHY

Andrus, Percy H. "Historical Markers and Memorials in Michigan." *Michigan History Magazine* 15 (Spring 1931): 167-374.

Armstrong, Tom, et al. *200 Years of American Art.* [Boston]; David R. Godine in association with the Whitney Museum, 1976.

The Art in City Hall. [Grand Rapids]; The Municipal Arts Commission, 1978.

Baxter, Albert. *History of the City of Grand Rapids, Michigan.* New York and Grand Rapids: Munsell & Company, Publishers, 1891; reprint ed., Grand Rapids: Grand Rapids Historical Society, 1974.

Burroughs, Clyde H. "Painting and Sculpture in Michigan." *Michigan History Magazine* 20 (Autumn 1936): 395-409 and 21 (Spring 1937): 39-54, 141-157.

Clark, Joel. "Changes They've Seen." *Grand Rapids Press,* 22 January 1978, Wonderland Magazine, pp. 7, 8, 33.

Craven, Wayne. *Sculpture in America.* New York: Crowell, 1968.

Dean, Andrea O. "Grand Rapids Becomes a Showplace for Using Sculpture in Public Places." *AIA Journal* (October 1976): 40-43. Reprinted in *Michigan Municipal Review* (June 1977): 100, 102, 112.

Doezma, Marianne and Hargrove, June. *The Public Monument and Its Audience.* Cleveland: The Cleveland Museum of Art, 1977.

Ekdahl, Janis. *American Sculpture.* Art and Architecture Information Guide Series, vol. 5. Detroit: Gale Research Co., 1977.

Forgey, Benjamin. "A New Vision: Public Places With Sculpture." *Smithsonian* 6 (October 1975): 50-57.

Friedlander, Lee. *The American Monument.* New York: The Eakins Press Foundation, 1976.

Gibson, Arthur Hopkin (comp.). *Artists of Early Michigan.* Detroit: Wayne State University Press, 1975.

Goode, James M. *The Outdoor Sculpture of Washington, D.C.* Washington, D.C.: Smithsonian Institution Press, 1974.

Grand Rapids Park Story. [Grand Rapids: n.d.].

Idema, James M. "Very Few Even Look at Them," *Grand Rapids Herald,* 24 October 1948, feature sec. pp. 1, 3.

Judd, Dorothy Leonard. *The Art and Architecture of Fountain Street Church.* [Grand Rapids]: The Centennial Program Committee of Fountain Street Church, 1969.

Marlin, William. "Sprucing Up a City." *Saturday Review,* 7 February 1976: pp. 50-52.

May, George S. (comp.). *Michigan Civil War Monuments.* Lansing: Civil War Centennial Observance Commission, 1965.

Morris, Robert. "Interview: Robert Morris." *Michigan Art Journal* 1 (September 1976): 3, 4, 10.

O'Doherty, Brian. "The Grand Rapids Challenge." *Art in America* 62 (January 1974): 78-79.

________ . "Public Art and the Government: A Progress Report." *Art in America* 62 (May-June 1974): 44-49.

Proske, Beatrice Gilman. *Brookgreen Gardens Sculpture.* New ed., rev. and enl. Brookgreen, South Carolina: Brookgreen Gardens, 1968.

Robinette, Margaret A. *Outdoor Sculpture, Object and Environment.* New York: Watson-Guptil Publications, 1976.

Robert Morris, Grand Rapids Project. Grand Rapids: Grand Rapids Art Museum, 1975.

Sculpture of a City: Philadelphia's Treasures in Bronze and Stone. New York: Walker Publishing Co., Inc., 1974.

Sculpture Off the Pedestal. Grand Rapids: Grand Rapids Art Museum, 1973.

Taft, Lorado. *The History of American Sculpture.* New ed. with a supplementary chapter by Adeline Adams. New York: The Macmillan Co., 1930.

Vrchota, Janet. "Grand Rapids Case Study." *Design and Environment* 5 (Summer 1974): 28-31.

NOTE

While the above have been helpful, much of the documentary material was collected in bits and pieces from a variety of sources including local and state libraries, archives, museums, interviews, and a field inventory. Source materials include an inventory form with bibliography and photograph for each sculpture; local, county, and state histories; newspaper and magazine articles; correspondence; photographs; and dedication booklets. All of the documentation will be housed in the Michigan State University Archives and Historical Collections, East Lansing, Michigan.

INDEX